A Gathering of
Grandmothers

A Gathering of Grandmothers

Words of Wisdom from Women of Spirit and Power

Lynne Namka, Ed.D.

"When the Grandmothers Speak,
the Earth will Heal."

Hopi Prophecy

Writers Club Press
San Jose   New York   Lincoln   Shanghai

A Gathering of Grandmothers
Words of Wisdom from Women of Spirit and Power

Writers Club Press
an imprint of iUniverse, Inc.

For information address:
iUniverse, Inc.
5220 S. 16th St., Suite 200
Lincoln, NE 68512
www.iuniverse.com

ISBN: 0-595-23990-0

Printed in the United States of America

Dedication and Acknowledgements

A Gathering of Grandmothers: Words of Wisdom from Women of Spirit and Power is dedicated to Mary Diamond, founder of the Grandmother's Gatherings group and Ann Kreilkamp, founder and editor of Crone Chronicles, A Journal of Conscious Aging.

I also dedicate this book to those four women who have formed much of whom I am: my mother, Rhea Olive Wickiser, my aunt, Margaret Nancy Heim and my two grandmothers, Olive Bell Fox and Lydia Denny Wickiser.

Thanks go to Judy Atwell, Phyllis Fredona, Mary Fredona and Bernie Brasfield for their help in editing this book. And thanks to my husband, Gordon Harnack, who designed the cover and without whose help this book could not have published. The cover graphic is adapted from a graphic in Microsoft's Design Gallery collection.

The articles Living Simply, Withering Face, Flowering Spirit, Transformation, The Call of the Crone, Who Is Crone?, Arrival of the Crone, Fullness: The Crone and Her Shadow, Seasons of Crone and Risk Taking at 101 were previously published in Crone Chronicles, A Journal of Conscious Aging.

All royalties from this book will be donated to The Gathering of Grandmothers and The International Council of Crones. For current activities on these two groups, do a web search.

CONTENTS

Dedication and Acknowledgements v
Introduction xv

Grandmother Tales: Woman As Storyteller

Wise Women Share Their Stories 3
Jump Up and Live 6
Shirley Tassencourt
Wise Women On Love and Loving 12
Grandmother Cave 14
Gaia Reblitz
Living Simply 22
Redmoonsong
Ancestral Dreaming 30
Gwendolyn Endicott
Sleeping Beauty 35
Shirley Dunn Perry
Message From The Goddess 37
Maya Levy

In The Beginning, We Were Daughters

We, the Girl Children of the Tribe, Find Our Own 45
My Mother Taught Me How To Pray 48
Geri Gilbert

Women in Paradox 50

Jane Evans

Mothers 54

Joyce A. Kovelman

I Am My Mother 56

Anonymous

On Becoming a Loose Woman

Seeking the Fluid Self 61

Wise Women on Change 65

What I Did On My Summer Vacation 67

Nana Gaia

Wise Women on Attachments 71

The Changing of the Tastes 73

June Keen

A Determined Strength, A Different Life 80

Joyce Kovelman

Wise Women on Moving Through Fear 84

"Now It Is My Turn," Said the Little Red Hen 86

Jane Evans

5 Ls to Live By 88

gael P. Mustapha

Journey to the Islands of the Galapagos 91

Lynne Namka

Withering Face, Flowering Spirit 93

Skye Blaine

Wise Women on the Joys of Being an Older Woman 96

The Old Crone

Yes to Croneship! 101

Look At Me—This Is Who I Am: The Charge of the Crone 104
Antiga

Transformation 105
Rucy Neiman

The Call of the Crone 106
Ann Kreilkamp

Baba Yaga 107
Antiga

Wise Women on Knowing the Dark Side 115

Arrival of the Crone 117
Persha Gertler

Fullness: The Crone and Her Shadow 119
Ann Kreilkamp

Grandmother Proverbs for the Second Half of Life 121

After The Menopause 123
Gwendolyn Purdy

Seasons of Crone 124
Dorothy L. Bray

Aged Bones—Supple Minds

The Gift of Contraction 131

Wise Women on Sorrow 134

On Youth 136
Anonymous

Ever-Changing Woman 137

Lynne Namka

Wise Women on Aging 138

Cause For Pause 140

Joan Weiss Hollenbeck

An Unlikely Friendship 141

Lynne Namka

Wise Women on Service to the World 148

As A Grandmother, I Write My Story 150

Anonymous

Saving What's Good 155

Angela Pechenpaugh

A Crabbit Old Woman Wrote This… 157

Wise Women On Releasing the Negative 159

Nana 161

Cathyann Fisher

Old Bones Secrets: Good Genes, Capacity to be Happy 162

gael P. Mustapha

Risk Taking at 101 166

Jean-Noel Bassior

The Gathering of the Grandmothers

When the Grandmothers Speak 175

Grandmother Crones Offer Solutions and Hope 177

Jan Gregg

An Anthem to Our Global Family 181

The Grandmothers at Cielo en Tierra

Council of Grandmothers 183

Gaia Reblitz

Wise Women on Spirituality 186
Clan Mother 188
Gaia Reblitz
Oath of the Clan Mothers 190
Joyce Kovelman
The Grandmothers Speak 191
The Art of Life 193
Joanna Miller
Wisdom Within 194
Mary Ann McClellan
Grandmother's Way 195
Gaia Reblitz
Ancient Prophecy 197
Lynne Namka

"This is the time to call the Grandmothers together in sacred circles. We Elders hold the memory of the past and a clear vision of the future. Our experience reflects a change in consciousness that gives birth to a new paradigm. As midwives, we Grandmothers need to support our continued growth as responsible members of the human family. With sorrow we see compassion and heart have been squeezed from our institutions. We are confronted by much pain and suffering. As we stand at the end of our lives, aware of death and new beginnings, our work is to heal and secure a future for our grandchildren."

From the meeting of the Grandmothers during the first Grandmother's group at Cielo en Tierra.

Introduction

Lynne Namka (author credit)

How do we older women—we, the grandmothers—make a positive impact on our world? The process starts by knowing ourselves as women of Spirit and Power. Then with sure voices, we can reach out to tell other women that they too can find their strong woman voice.

Women's change down through the ages has always come from the center. Since the beginning of humans huddling together to keep off the fear and darkness of the night, fire has collected and held dear the healing stories of priestesses, shamans, goddesses, medicine women and those of the ordinary women, formed by the sweat of their brows and the salt of their tears. Clear, centered women have always passed ideas down from the hearth, the campfire, the meetinghouse, the sewing circle on to the neighbors, the community and the world at large.

We start with our own stories—calling forth our personal folk tales. Telling one's story helps women birth themselves through personal mythology—a tapestry that is uniquely one's own. In this process, women create their own myths by telling varied stores of their lives. Older women often turn to symbols within these tales for richness and depth. The myths that older women weave are filled with transformative symbols, which arise from the unconscious mind. The symbols are chosen on an unconscious level reflecting unresolved themes and patterns of the woman's life, which are to be played through. In this tapestry women weave old metaphors, archetypes and reoccurring themes from ancient legends, fairy tales and the literature of our world to round out their myths.

Symbols hasten the alchemical process of the later years as they bypass logic and reason and spring from the richness and depth of imagination.

The purpose of woman's alchemy is to satisfy the deep hunger inside of rescuing the soul. Elizabeth Howe and Shelia Moon describe the hunger for symbols in women's lives: "By our symbols we shall be known. They carry and express our uniqueness and our ordinariness. They impart to life its bright or dark imaginativeness.... As soon as we look into the mirror of the waters we are face to face with the multiplicity of our being—best to worst—by way of symbols. And if the 'all' is to be used toward a wholeness of living and loving, religiously meaningful life need to be based on symbolic life made conscious." Symbols and metaphors help women organize their lives by conjuring up personal meaning.

Some women break through the cultural patterns of subservience and low expectations. Some women break free from the rigid expectations of society that they become a second-class citizens. Some learn to know themselves and live rich, unconventional lives. What kind of programming and belief systems did they overcome in order to become themselves? How have these uncommon women freed themselves from the bonds of a culture that overtly and subtly tells them not to be themselves and to take the lesser role?

A Gathering of Grandmothers: Wisdom from Elder Women of Spirit and Power addresses these questions about becoming one's self. Our book is about women celebrating women. The authors are older women who have found richness in life and are aging with zest and enthusiasm with much to share. It is a collection of, stories, poems, healing ways, rituals, dreams and visions, fairy tales, wise sayings. It speaks to the rite of passage of women moving into the second half of life with grace and wisdom. The stories are about women moving into their feminine Elderhood as they find their individual and collective voices. The emotional language of our feminine Elderhood is one of celebration. Our book is a collection of stories of energy and empowerment.

Older women who speak out about empowerment, conscious aging and growing old with spirit and fire are to be honored and celebrated. Our authors are gutsy women who have waited a lifetime living, collecting and gathering their ancestral stories. Now they pass them on to you in the hopes that you too will write your own unique story.

Grandmother Tales: Woman As Storyteller

"Love and you will find your own poet's voice in your own throat connected
to your own heart and your own mind and you use it well."

~Leslea Newman

WISE WOMEN SHARE THEIR STORIES

Lynne Namka

"Oral exchanges among women in groups, caring and talking to one another, will create a new dealing for women in which they invite and invent life."

Carolyn Heilbaum

The telling of women's tales is one of the oldest forms of human communication, which began around campfires as the older women instructed younger ones in the ways of the clan. Storytellers present the living tradition of the values of being human. Women's stories and tales preserve the folk wisdom passed down from one generation to the next. Woman's stories, as told to us in verse, fairy tales, ritual or prose, are instrumental in shaping our own lives. For stories are living tradition. Each teller of tales adds her own piece, her own personality while preserving the ancient wisdom.

The time of the Feminine Elder is characterized by the metaphor of the Wise Old Woman who knows her own wisdom and sacredness. Sound mental health in older individuals is related to moving from an egocentric perspective to a broader worldview of service. The eldering process is a time of quiet servitude where women come forward, gaining greater knowledge so that they in turn may pass it on. It allows us to move from the helpless, ailing older woman as an archetype to the strong woman archetype. Archetypes are commonly identified patterns of human experience that reoccur through history. Too often negative archetypes of the older woman evoke an emotional response and contribute to prejudice and bigotry.

The strong older woman archetype presents the Elder woman as the heroine of her own story. Age becomes Sage. The Sage represents a living symbol of the potential that lies within the woman of later years. Her story relates her own transformational journey as she grows in wisdom following the biddings of her unconscious mind. As Jungian analyst, Marie Louise von Franz said, "Fairy tales are parables of our own journey through life." And we all know on an inner level that a fairy tale a day keeps the dragons away—our own inner dragons of fear and despair.

Carl Jung wrote of the alchemical process and the use of symbols and fantasy that help transform life's pain into self-understanding. When women move into their center they find richness and depth that sustain their psyche on a deep emotional chord. Jung said, "(Wo)man is in need of a symbolic life.... Only the symbolic life can express the need of the soul." The creative unconscious energies in us awaken our fantasy and needed symbols to create a space for personal development. Women's stories are lush and nourishing; they are the stuff of which we feed our lives when all else goes wrong.

Mythical consciousness bids us return to fairy tales to reclaim the magic and innocence of our youth. Fairy tales from the world mythology describe the Feminine Elder in archetypical ways. Positive archetypes are the Fairy Godmother, the Wise Old Woman, and the Old Crone, and the understanding mother who encourages her daughter to be her own person. Unfortunately there are not too many examples of older women who seek and find strength for themselves. The negative archetypes, which are plentiful, include the Weak Mother, the Wicked Step Mother, the Poor Old Woman and the Old Hag. The woman who is vain, greedy and obsessed with finding love is another common theme. Older women have the opportunity to work through these negative archetypes and inner shadows in their lives as they come closer to the end of the alchemical journey.

Old stories are being retold today from the woman's point of view, providing a broader perspective of the ancient wisdom handed down from one generation to another. We pull from the deep well of wisdom to step back and look at the meanings of the aging process. Our stories give us new hats to try, new clothes to put on and the choice of new roles to play. In later life, women begin to reclaim those missing stories to bring back those missing pieces of themselves.

Reading about other women's stories gives us models of finishing our business with our parents. They help us finish earlier versions of ourselves and move on. Women's stories help us pay old debts to ourselves and provide symbols of rebirth. They can become the touchstone for developing meaning. They work on us at an unconscious level shaping our psyche. They help us move past the clutter and give life meaning and substance. Women's stories are sacred as they speak to us of our own interconnectedness and our personal empowerment. Besides retelling the tales of old, it is now up to us to live out our stories and write them.

There are many unanswered questions around which to base our stories. What role models do we women have for growing older successfully and happily? What illusions do we need to dispel? What can we discard along the way? With what metaphors do we define ourselves? What adventures can we play through? And what stories do we need to hear and tell ourselves so that we can reclaim those last aspects of ourselves? What would the fairy tale of our lives look like? What form will the birth of our personal mythology take? How does our story interconnect with those of others who formed and shaped us? How do they connect with those of our ancestral line who follow us? Questions, always questions which bring forth the retort, "Ah, but that's another story."

We women have so much weaving yet to do while we spin our stories. So come, join our circle. As we embrace our feminine Elderhood, our vintage is to age into wisdom. Our stories lead us there. So come Sisters, come close into our circle. Listen with your ears, your hearts, and your deep feminine soul. Come closer, the story spirits have much to tell us. Let the stories begin!

JUMP UP AND LIVE

Shirley Tassencourt

In 1976, after the separation; after 27 years of caretaking of the husband, the kids, the animals (all of whom I loved) the guests, the relatives, washing the clothes and the dishes, matching the socks, cooking the food, mending illnesses, hurt feelings and frustrations, going to meetings and the incessant driving until someone became sixteen years of age, circle after circle, starting at the home in the morning, returning to the home by day, by night; circles repeating, repeating, now the way of the householder was over.

The kids were over 20 and into their own lives when I read the "Goodbye, it's been swell" note on the table. The house was empty of love, so why stay? As I walked out the wide open door I began humming as little sparks of joy came rushing in. I felt like the Greek slave who could leave the gloom of Rome and return to his wind swept divine temples. I was no longer beholden to anyone but the One upstairs. I began to giggle. This had possibilities. To myself, "Well Dad, what a way to say goodbye after 27 years but thanks anyway old pal, old rat." I exuded indignation and gratitude and great excitement. "Fly Baby, fly."

That year I taught art at a private school. They objected to my wearing blue jeans to teach art and pottery. I submitted an article as to how the President of the United States was wearing Levis for anything less than state occasions. Didn't work. I left. 'Baby' was flying further.

When we divided the bed linen and all, I received the island property with the fourteen-foot cabin and monies from half of the modest suburban house. By becoming a contractor and worker, I turned those monies and the small cabin into a full house. Happily I had grown up on a street with ten boys, so I knew what not to do with subcontractors. Being an artist I had a wide latitude in using interesting recycled materials. New tools, new media but, what the heck—another art project.

Two years later, there it stood—1500 square feet of solar passive house-ness, three stories shingled by yours truly, all tucked into the hillside. What satisfaction, what amazement, what a cosmic joke. Women of the world, we can do it!

A dozen years later I had a destiny vision of sitting on the desert floor covered with dirt, dirt as far as I could see. Around the same time I got a message from my Peralandra garden that it was going west—and I should come too. I did. The island land purchased twenty years before had appreciated in value. There was the pension, insurance and all the goodies I'd never acquired just because I'd risked the impossible—building my own house, I had the means to go west.

Here was the wherewithal to go west and become, what? A desert dirt-ball? Wherewithal eventually bought beautiful land in Texas Canyon in Arizona where the great boulders are strewn as if by giants. Women's affinity for the spiritual is perhaps our major gift to society. The fact that we don't incarnate as deeply as men allows us to "lift off" a bit and be awash in spirit more easily. The spiritual underpinnings that took me on my western adventure started at a dinner the night before flying to Arizona to give a workshop on "clay and spirit." A friend inquired about my attraction to the southwest. The words that came were as astonishing to me as to her, "I'm going to find my sacred spot." My eyes opened wide. I listened, "I'm going to inhabit it." I opened my mouth in amazement again. Then I said. "That's all."

The following year, 1992, I spent six weeks at a ranch near Benson, Arizona making a fifteen foot rammed earth sculpture. Chipping away on forty-three tons of earth, I soon became the archetypal dirt ball I'd envisioned. I fell in love with the part of Arizona called Texas Canyon that sports a big boulder field some hundreds of feet high. In the afternoons I wandered among the giant rocks totally entranced. The boulders make hundreds of first-rate natural sculptures. That I would soon live within hugging distance of such fabulous stone monuments was beyond my dreaming.

One morning drumming the sun up at a Stonehenge type configuration, I heard chanting. No one was around. Wow. An hour later I met a woman realtor who was looking for sacred land to put it in a "forever trust." "I think you have found it," I said. "I think you are on it. Maybe I heard the chanting so I could tell you." A year later, the real estate woman called me to tell me of land for sale in the Texas Canyon area with rocks and a "presence."

In January of 1993, three elder women, Liz Campbell, Allegra Ahlquist and I were following a realtor around thirty acres of beautiful land, Texas Canyon land, in breathless suspense. We knew we couldn't divide the land and although almost strangers, we became tenants in common by the end of the walk. As caretakers of the medicine circle we never suspected how ceremony and attunement would open our hearts and senses to the beautiful Mother Earth and the ever-changing paintings of Father Sky. We dedicated ourselves to work in concert with the beings, visible and invisible, of the land. Turning around, we saw a double rainbow. It stayed an hour, a true affirmation of our offering. We are honored to be caretakers of this land that truly belongs to the Apache nation here at the foot of Cochise's Stronghold.

A month later, Allegra came to the land settlement having gotten a divination about the land from a Mayan Jaguar Priest. He called the land Whirling Yellow Sprout where new life will come. The divination awakened our sensitivities to the use and alignment of the land. One caution was not to hurt, not to fear the rattlesnakes but to feed them jade and turquoise and make a shrine in the rocks. We did this ceremony the day after settlement. Coming back to our wilderness property and hidden shrine two days later, we found a tall blue Macaw feather sticking in a tuft of grass in the middle of the shrine. No one else knew of the shrine, which is really in the boonies. We called the Mayan Priest with our message of shock. He said, "The land is telling you that it is pleased with what you do." Macaw parrots are not native to Arizona. The Macaw parrot plume was the sacred feather of the Mayans.

Spirit has sent five teachers to heal this land here at the foot of the Dragoon Mountains, the battleground of the last century between Cochise's Apaches and the United States Cavalry. Many gifts were sought and brought to the land. A visiting Lumi Shaman burned cedar and offered prayers in my dome shelters. When he finished, he said, "I'm happy to meet the old ones." I asked, "You mean the invisible ones?" "Yes, they are pleased with what you are doing—greeting the sun, prayer, appreciation, ceremony. They are telling me they talk to you. But you don't talk back. It bothers them." He began to school me about this.

Last spring the Mayan Jaguar Priest conducted a three-day puberty rite in the ancient Mayan way here at Whirling Yellow New Life. We all felt the power channeled into the individual from the tribe and the gift of the individual to the group—the circle of mutual indebtedness. Again land was blessed as eighty-five guests woke up to something terribly missing in our western culture.

We asked the spirit of the land to allow us to work in concert with it and throw away control patterns right and left. Poetess M. C. Richards says, "Everything is love and danger." Well when we three women moved in risk and mutuality, a fifteen-acre natural medicine wheel became evident. Boulders straddled the four directions. Four large "stone people" boulders standing eight to ten feet high scribbled a circle in the center finishing off a sacred hoop. The sacred hoop is now a park and our shelters are on the back of the fifteen acres. A crystal field of white quartz underlines the wheel as well as our residences.

A year after the land was purchased, I began the first bagged earth dome after attending a one-day workshop with Nadar Kalili. The passionate teaching of architect Kalili was "Take earth from the ground, take work from your hands, make shelter for your bodies." Matriculating at the

University of MUD, we learned the art of corbeling domes. Big upside bowls to live in—a proper late life shelter for a potter, I'd say. We laid circle upon circle of bags filled with moist dirt and lowly the beautiful curve of the dome happened.

The potter in me came out to help sculpt my new home. I hired a backhoe, three people and commenced to build an eighteen-foot earth dome. My nineteen-year-old grandson came to help with the first dome, and then became foreman for the second and larger dome. A great joy for grandmother. We stacked straw bales to make a stair scaffolding to hoist the fifty-pound bags. At sixty-eight years of age, I filled bags of dirt but didn't lift them. I cemented, stuccoed and sculpted while the young'uns did the labor.

My destiny vision was correct. I became dirt for the next year. It all felt familiar to me, the potter—these great upside down bowls to live in. The first dome took three months to finish. Five months later, we finished a larger dome of twenty-four feet in diameter. The beautiful curve of the domes happened. Coreling and corbelling, the workers found the stance of the big upside down pot using the eye of a tennis player and the sensitivities of an accomplished potter. There was such joy in realizing the big forms that looked like the giant boulders rolling around the land.

Dome I has a cupola on top in the loft room spilling out to a 360 degree view for viewing the electrical storms, sunsets and the sky moods that transform this ancient land of Cochise and Gerinomo. The loft is for writing and downstairs is the meditation room and ceremonial space and we call it Domosophia. People ask me if I live alone and I say no adding, "There's Joey the white Samoyed dog." But to myself I say, "There is the "Saint" and the "old ones.""

Dome II houses the facilities—combination dining room and kitchen with a small bath and the loft functions as the bedroom and is called Domicile. The first nine feet of walls are doubled making them forty inches thick. The windows of domes are necessarily arched, the entrances are great vaults. I live in a great castle feeling the twelfth century breathing on my neck. These thick walled domes keep a mean temperature so heating and cooling are minimal. A wood stove for an hour on cold nights does it. Domes don't collapse in earthquakes, dissolve in floods, burn in fires, blow over in winds or harbor critters in walls. Cancel insurance!

Domicile II is topped by a seven-foot wide, five-foot high crystal skylight under which I lie watching Orion chase the Pleiades nightly. What a gift to open up the love life between the night sky and myself after a lifetime of ceilings. You can see I'm hunkering down for the curious new times. Sunlight reflects off the big crystal pyramid skylight and lamplight shines out at night. Allegra calls the dome shelter a lighthouse. I say, "Yes and I'm waiting for the shoreline to arrive."

My garden has gone west and blooms profusely six months of the year. I have gone west and bloom twelve months of the year. I pinch myself. Is this really true? Everyday is Saturday. The air is like champagne. I sleep looking at stars. Folks come and we meditate, we dance, we drum, we sing, we pray. I have found my sacred spot. I inhabit it. And that is all. As a child once asked, "God, how come you give me this?"

Listening to my vision led me here so risk wasn't an issue. Fun in finding form got those buildings up plus the over-arching power that brought those workers here. "Go for your bliss," said Joseph Campbell and I did. "Feed yourself on joy," said the Buddha and I do. "Jump up and live," says the Mayan Jaguar Priest.

"What else, you betcha." I say.

Wise Women On Love and Loving

Age does not protect you from love. But love, to some extent, protects you from age.

Jeanne Moreau

What I cannot love, I overlook. Is that real friendship?

Anais Nin

If only one could tell true love from false love as one can tell mushrooms from toadstools.

Katherine Mansfield

It is not the love that people cannot respond to, it is the anxiety and desperation with the love, which people feel like the grasp of a drowning person... The love, the quiet, sure, unpossessive love they can respond to... So like a good chemist, extract anxiety from love and you will have a happy reciprocal love. Separate the fear from the love. Examine what caused the fear and anxiety. You'll win.

Anais Nin

Love doesn't just sit there, like a stone, it has to be made like bread; remade all the time, made new.

Ursula LeGuin

The truth [is] that there is only one terminal dignity—love. And the story of love is not important—what is important is that one is capable of love. It is perhaps the only glimpse we are permitted of eternity.

Helen Hayes

Because of its unconsciousness, the beginning of a relationship may be as naive as kittens at play, but if it is to become a real relatedness, it will require some serious effort... The objective is to clear a bridge freed from both egocentric distortion and compulsive over adaptation, across which free communication may pass and so permit two simple human beings to experience themselves, each other and the maximum current of life that belongs in the situation between them. In this way love and meaning unite in a life experience which is not only personal, but also, in a deeper sense, truly religious.

Eleanor Bertine

Love is the form that gives life to the process and is itself increased by its own endeavor. Love becomes quite literally all. In states of coherence one is marrying oneself on all levels. Love then takes the most quantum leap and one loves all others in one's immediate reality. This then moves to an all-encompassing Love of all and everything. And so love becomes the most gentle and most powerful agent for the fielding and forming of reality. In love the lenses fall away. In love one forms all forming... In love one arrives home at last.

Jean Houston

GRANDMOTHER CAVE

Gaia Reblitz

She had made a commitment to her inner voice. All that she needed now rode on her back: water, a little food, a sleeping roll, warm clothing for the night which might carry snow so late in fall and at such altitude.

With a deep breath and a tremor in her heart, she took in her surroundings. Sun patterns lay on the ground, shivering with the slight sighing of the wind. In front of her opened a clearing, a turn around made for logging trucks. Like an ache it reminded her of the civilization she had left behind for a day, of the trade-in of natural beauty for material comfort, of the sacrifice of the wild and the feminine side of life. Shrubs bordered the open space and behind them, to her right, rose tall and ancient trees. Stretching her sight across the wound in the land she touched deep green ridges and a snowcapped mountain peak in the distance, center of a wilderness.

Already, the layers of her being were falling.

She turned to her right into a forest trail. As she passed the portal of tall and ancient trees, she stopped to speak a prayer. She wanted to give thanks for the special moment and ask for permission to enter. As a gift she left some tobacco. Peace beyond understanding welcomed her—and she thought she could not bear it. Then she turned around in a full circle to unwind from her old self, gathered her courage and started on the journey.

Some last huckleberries caught her attention, and gratefully she picked a few. They were manna to her, power food from the Mother. With the sweet, tart, juicy flesh she drew into her a new strength and a healing. It made her feel full, as if she had eaten a whole meal.

14

She thought of her children with whom she had enjoyed many nature walks. When they were mere toddlers, she had begun to introduce them to wild foods—to miner's lettuce and chickweed, dandelion, nettles and sorrel, to seasonal berries and mushrooms. Teaching her children, she had learned how deeply the gathering woman lived inside her, as an essence of her soul, a root.

As she walked down the path, trees enclosed her like the pillars of a sacred temple. They were formidable energy, aloof, yet firmly grounded. They played with the winds, with sunlight, stars and moon. They communed with the earth in sigh and song and deep embrace while they drank in the waters of life and the love of the Mother. She felt the patience and power and the ageless wisdom with which the trees drew heaven and earth together, magicians of alignment, messengers between this planet and the universe, and beyond.

Gently she touched one, its rough bark etching feelings into her fingers, sending warmth, connection, and alertness. Then she hugged one fiercely, never wanting to let go. It was so full of life and vibrant peace. It seemed to hold joy and the pain, freedom and commitment in equal measure, distilled into a harmony beyond human understanding. She opened herself fully and felt her heart beat in unison with the pulse of the tree and the rhythm of the earth.

Remembering her journey, she moved back onto the path. Whenever fears crept up about being out here alone, in this unknown wilderness, she hummed and sang to come back to center. And so she hiked among the Standing People. Whispers rose and fell, punctuated by sounds of creaking and cracking. Once in a while she heard the flutter and eerie call of a bird. Louder though than anything else rang in her the immense stillness of the ancient forest. In this dim, cool, moist holiness she shrank away, leaving her heart exposed and expanding. It seemed such a long time ago, since she had been in touch with her own people and had done her daily routine, had laughed and argued, worked, cared for family and friends, had struggled and cried. Softly her feet drummed on the earth,

putting her into a trance. She firmed her step and increased the beat, in
need of feeling her own presence.

Dipping and rising, the trail skirted the foot of a mountain. As the land
sloped down from her right, small streams came tumbling across her path,
forming magic pools and miniature islands, exposing multicolored rocks
and nursing little gardens along the banks. When she reached a fork in the
trail she turned right to begin the ascent. Like a sleepy snake the path
wound its way up the steep mountainside, across mossy rivulets and
through thinning forests. Huge cliffs grew out of the depth to her left,
immense smooth walls, which towered above her and fell away below to a
valley hidden from view. Her heart stopped at the sight, and part of her
was ready to run. For there was power sweeping towards her, and with it
rode a wave of fear.

Breathe, she told herself. Be still.

Her senses scanned the place and knew that it contained some mystery,
some hidden treasure. Was this what she was looking for? Without much
thought she climbed down a jumble of loose rocks and tried to skirt the
cliff face. But there was no path, and the slope became dangerous. So she
clambered back to the trail and was led up into an open landscape where
sparse sagebrush and a few dwarfed junipers grew among boulders. In the
middle of the path sat a cryptic sign, etched into one of the rocks. Friends
had left it for her as a guidepost. It meant: stop, turn left, and look for a
hidden trail.

Just a few minutes later she found herself standing at the edge of a small
plateau, drinking in the spectacular sight. All around her, nearly full circle,
stretched wild, majestic mountains. She felt like an eagle perched on the
rock, surveying her range with keen eye and total attention. That she
stood right on top of the cave, occurred to her much later, in retrospect.

A huge medicine wheel with a double ring had been laid out to the left
of her lookout, and some of the stones had lost their place. Respectfully
she closed the circles and straightened the spokes. Then she sat down in

the south, the place of trust and innocence, for a time of meditation and thanksgiving. Another layer of her came loose, and she sighed with relief.

Softly she sang a song to greet this holy place and introduce herself. How magic this journey, she thought. Everything so special, so full of meaning, so natural and simple. Counter pointing such high feelings, her body reminded her that it was time for lunch. There was no real hunger, but a need to ground herself with some familiar routine. Lounging on a bed of needles among a stand of small firs, she nibbled some food, canned fish, rice cakes, and a few dried fruits and nuts.

Then she gathered her things and dropped down the slope on the other side of the plateau into a thicket. She had to climb over fallen trees, skirt around bushes and duck through branches, as she followed her wide-open instinct telling her that she was on the right track. A low stone barrier brought her to a halt. Across it, she spotted a very fine line. It wound down and over a steep stony slope, disappearing behind the cliff wall. Over loose shale she followed the path. And as she turned towards the rock face, a huge gaping mouth came into view.

Around the triangle of the entrance lay a natural garden, accented by a few tall trees. Feeling awed and infinitely small, she offered tobacco and some of her hair to ask for admittance, and then she tiptoed into the sanctuary. The damp floor of the cave was covered with fine volcanic red stones, and in many places a carpet had been spread of luscious green plants and tiny white starflowers. Terraces led back into the depth, and the soft sound of water drew her in. Her eyes adjusted to the dim light and she saw that the back wall was overgrown with moss. Through the tangled web dripped a crystal clear spring. Then it moved on and out and down the mountainside. With reverence she let the drops fall into her hands and drank the cool, delicious sacred water of life.

The little basin, sculpted into the stone floor in long and patient labor, became her sacred place. Around its edge she laid out a few things for an altar: sage and cedar, a medicine bundle, a feather, a crystal. Then she sat down for a song and a prayer. And almost instantly she fell apart.

Sobs welled up and in wild abandon she began to cry. Nameless anguish burst out of her. It seemed to rise from the depth of the earth, from the forests around her and out of the wide expanse of the universe, mixing with her own heartaches and losses and fears. All of her world, on the inside and outside, called for purification, and willingly she gave herself over to the task. Together, they cried for a long time.

The power of the cave had broken her heart open, leaving no escape, no retreat, and no boundaries. Diving into the flood of emotions, she embraced each feeling and gave it voice. She knew herself safe here, protected, unjudged, and even appreciated. After a while, she almost enjoyed the experience, this clearing channels and draining bogs, so that life could run freely again.

Human voices broke into her world. She found barely time to compose herself, before two young men, loudly talking, tramped into the cave. The sudden noise hit her psyche like a whip, and she wanted to fade into the cavern walls but a sense of danger roused her and caused her to act in an instant to cover her vulnerability. She wiped her face, put on a social mask and stepped out of the dark to greet the men. To her surprise her voice sounded firm and friendly, drawing the visitors into small time conversation and welcoming them with a cup of the cave's spring water. The men poked around for a little while, but when they found that there were no other chambers to the cave, they left the same way they had come from. She could hear them hollering all the way down the trail far below. She relaxed with a sigh and as she remembered the bewildered look, when they had first caught sight of her, she chuckled, and then she laughed out loud.

Light was fading fast. She spread a sleeping bag in a dry and even spot where she could enjoy a full view of the great snowy mountain across the valley. A sharp cold came streaming in from the opening, and she lost her resolve to stay up through the night, praying for a vision. She felt exhausted emotionally and the unexpected visit had jolted her back into an uncomfortable reality. For a moment she even considered packing up and hiking out. But the dark would catch up with her long before she could reach her car. You committed yourself to a night out here, she told herself. Don't give up now.

And so she donned every piece of clothing she had brought, added some items to her altar and picked up her rattle one more time. She felt such a relief to be alone again and safe. "Thank you, Mother Earth, for your protection. And thank you for my life and all its many gifts." Her gratitude spilled over, as she named every blessing she knew and remembered all the people to who she was connected. From her thoughts and words rose a chant, a childlike song to life.

She danced in slow circles around the cave and gave thanks for the sacred space, for the welcome and for the patience for which her tears had been accepted. She felt healed and free-and the earth seemed to consent with a deep sigh. Into the empty, tired place inside, which her crying had carved, flowed now a sense of peace and wholeness. And she sat down by the altar, moved into that inner cave and became still.

When she got up, she traced the walls of the rock chamber with her fingers in silent, loving communion and with great respect. Then she leaned by the entrance to sing a song to the land and to draw up strength for the night. There was, and might always be, a part in her quivering with fright. Crossing her arms over her belly, she hugged it and kept it from taking over.

Before darkness fell and the stars came out, she drew with tobacco a circle of safekeeping around her sleeping place and lay down. She looked over to the mountain, so powerfully still. Then she gazed up into the maze of the ceiling, and let herself be drawn into patterns and figures and stories. Quieting her mind, she prayed and asked for guidance in her sleep. Then, to the lullaby of gently dripping waters, she fell asleep.

It was a fitful night. Animals rustled about, and strange droning and shifting sounds kept waking her, coming from deep within the cave and from above. They raised every dragon of fear in her, and a few times she had to pray really hard to stay sane. But somehow she never lost faith that she was protected, that this was a Grandmother cave who held her lovingly in her womb. She could feel the energy of the earth nurturing and strengthening her all through the night, bringing her home to herself. Sometimes she caught glimpses of spirits standing close by and watching over her. They seemed to tell her stories, of sacred ceremonies held long ago, of water rituals affirming a bond between the source here and healing springs far down in the valley.

Moving in and out of dreams, she remembered later only fragments, but those in vivid detail: A herd of buffalo came walking towards her, and at the last moment they opened up their ranks in two lines and surrounded her completely. She just stood there, watching in fascination, apparently without fear. Another scene showed her a brightly lit fire pit, rimmed with a circle of sculptures. Some seemed carved of wood, others of stone. They looked to her like sacred images, god and goddess symbols. Young people, and she thought she recognized her sons among them, played around the fire and were beginning to smash the wooden figures. Knowing that the stone sculptures would survive, she stood by without great concern. She was sad, that the symbols had to go.

Twittering woke her with a start, as a band of bats flew out of the recessed cave. She sat up straight, then relaxed and smiled. Dawn was breaking, and she felt great, renewed. What she had dreaded as a "night of fear" had become a night of rebirth. In the eerie morning light the great mountain across the entrance sent greetings to her, taking on many faces, speaking messages which she could not grasp with her mind, but understood somewhere deep within her body. She felt blessed and just lay there, watching the sky. From gray-blue it brightened to turquoise and became marbled with orange. Finally the sun flared up over the ridge to the left of the peak. With clammy fingers and ecstasy in her heart, she captured the moment in a drawing. Then she went over to the little pool to give thanks.

Packrats had kept busy during the night, taking medicines off her altar, including a fair-sized bundle, and leaving a few stones neatly in their place. She felt happy with the exchange. To her it was a sign that the spirits of the place had accepted her, claiming a little giveaway. She left another present for them in a niche. Then she asked the cave for permission to take some healing water and a red stone back home. For balance she offered tobacco and sang a last song. Then she packed her bags and hiked out.

A thin blanket of snow lay over the land, fading under the sun's steady gaze. She climbed straight to the top of the cave to explore different perspectives and to bask in the world's and her own newness. When she turned a corner, she met with two friends who had just hiked in. Together they looked out over the mountains and watched in silence as a pair of eagles circled above.

LIVING SIMPLY

Redmoonsong

"This is my job! This is my sacred path."

We have a responsibility to transform the world. Everything we do in our everyday lives affects everything that's going on all the time. The personal is the political. I cannot separate my spirituality from my use of resources. I'm trying to get simpler and simpler. The word sacrifice means to sanctify. I want every aspect of my life sacred.

There is a balance between having enough food but not have so much that we get unhealthy. There's a balance between having a shelter but not having a shelter that's polluting, taking so much work that you have to have somebody else clean up after you. We need to find these balances in our lives. I tell people, "Don't keep what you can't care for. I mean care. I don't mean someone else caring for it. I mean *you, personally*, caring for it."

I've studied philosophy all of my life; on my own, because I didn't go to college. I was one of the few kids in Catholic school who actually read the Bible. I've always been looking for philosophy, for some kind of integration—even though all of the craziness in my 20's, and drugs and kids and affairs and guns and whatever else I was involved in.

When I was thirty-two, I moved to Ann Arbor, Michigan. I went into a food co-op and was suddenly thrust into an environment where I actually had the opportunity to practice the philosophy I had studied. I found a way—an alternative lifestyle that integrated my philosophy of living with wholeness and practical application. My life was changed by the people I met there. I consider Ann Arbor, Michigan, my spiritual birthplace.

I was actually able to learn how to practice what I preached. I had a philosophy of non-violence and simple living, and now I had a methodology for practicing that. For me that kind of integrity is a path to power. It's my path to power. If you set your whole life up so you are practicing every day everything you believe in, the source of power is continually in you. It's continually operating!

In Ann Arbor, from the time I was 32 until I was 40, I finished raising my kids. They were teenagers then. I worked in food co-ops, I learned the skills of operating in the non-profit sector: how to fund raise; how to write grants; how to do collective decision making and cooperative decision making; how to start a food co-op from scratch. I taught people. I went into the schools. I taught kids how to grow sprouts and how to do vegetarian foods. I did all kinds of things in the community full-time.

I was learning these skills while I was finishing raising my kids, because I didn't know what I was going to do when my kids were grown. I got pregnant at 17, so it seemed like I always had kids. I had all three of them before I was 22. My whole life was governed by my children. I was divorced. I was a single mom for eleven years, from 1974 to 1985. When they were 18, I said, "You're out of here! This is my life now, 'cause I've done 23 years with you and I love you, but now it's my time." They all take care of themselves. They don't ever come home to me, 'cause I don't have a home. This happened at the age of 40. Tough love is useful: my kids do their own thing. They don't depend on me for anything, and they're happy with the work that I'm doing.

All of us have enormously precious energy to contribute, and so much of it is siphoned off. We think we've got to buy stuff for our grand kids. My kids don't expect nothin' from me, except advice—if they ask for it. I'm the only person they can find to ask these questions of them: "What is your highest good? What is justice in your life?" I say, "This is my job, as parent: to continue to nudge you toward wholeness; to point out paths of integrity and justice. You can choose to take them or not."

I went to a little log cabin in Oregon. I'd never been alone in my life. Here I was, in my 40th year in this little tiny cabin in southern Oregon in winter. I'd just sit there, fifteen hours a day. I'd chop my own wood. I'd haul my own water from the river and drink right out of the river. I had to hitchhike 15 miles to get my mail and I had to walk at least five miles to hitchhike. I was way back in there. It was dark and it was raining most of the time. It was a totally different experience for me—wonderful! I distributed stuff for the food co-op. I caused all kinds of trouble—I do that wherever I go, ask a lot of questions and then leave.

People love to see me come and they love to see me go. I provide this hit of intense energy. It's difficult to be with and I understand that, so my role is just this little spark thing, and then I split. I come back next year so they can do something with whatever was suggested.

I have been on the road ten years. I feel really lucky to be 50 and feel comfortable sleeping anywhere, any time, with no problems—sharing resources. That is a real gift, one that I've had to force myself to do. I was not raised like that; I was raised middle-class, only child. I was supposed to be a professional. Fortunately I got pregnant and became a professional mother. I managed to avoid a lot of stuff that equates my labor with money.

My movement toward radical feminism: I worked on Sonia Johnson's political campaign in 1984, when she ran for President on the Citizen's Party Ticket. Sonia Johnson is the ex-Mormon who wrote a book called *From Housewife to Heretic*. That's when I became a radical feminist. Before that I was certainly a feminist, thought I still gave primary support to men emotionally and sexually. I remember specifically when I became a radical feminist. We were talking about yin and yang. Sonia said to me, "Fuck yin and yang! A thousand years of foot-binding is all you have to know." It went BAM! for me, right then and there. I was the token heterosexual on her staff. Then I did have an affair with a young woman for a couple of weeks and they were all so happy with me!

I lived on a farm in Texas doing permaculture. In 1993-94 I was fortunate enough to spend a year and a half in Washington, D.C., and immerse myself in my racism by being partnered with a very militant black street man. I really had to confront my hidden racism. My partner before that was also African-American, but he was middle class. It's amazing that class differences are much more important that racial differences by a long shot. I learned a lot there. It was extremely painful.

I love Hershey's kisses with almonds, but I only like them frozen. So I'm going to get on the road, I'm going to get away from all of those dammed freezers, because I don't like them if they're not frozen. I tell people: fine-tune your addictions. If you're addicted to coffee and you don't want to be, then begin to get more and more discriminating about the kind of coffee you're going to drink, so that it might get to the point were it's fresh-roasted, French roast, ground beans, fresh with real cream…whatever you need to do to make yourself more conscious. People to, "Oh don't be so hard on yourself." I say, "This is my work."

The seeds of The Grandmother Speaks Walks formed when I was in D.C. I realized that I didn't want to walk across the country. I felt that grandmother energy is about local stuff. It's about bioregions. I've been involved in bioregionalism since 1980. The walks were more about slowing down, being outside all the time, changing habit patterns, looking at the power of the old woman, and about the speaking of the grandmother.

I had started going to Rainbow Gatherings trying to find Rainbow Grandmothers because I thought all these folks from the '60's were hip. In the '60's I was having kids. I was living with a straight husband. I missed the '60's. I bring that energy to this life now, as an Elder, as a Crone.

One of the Women's communities in Ohio is called The Susan B. Anthony Memorial Unrest Home. This is for old women! There's another called Spinster Haven, in Fayetteville, Arkansas—this is a very strong community for old women and women with disabilities. I think we are going to be seeing more and more women pooling resources to create space for women.

The poorer people are, the more you have to have extended networks. The more privileged you are, the more money you make, the more you can withdraw into your own private world—which makes us crazy! We are meant to live in community. It seems like not having much money is the only way you can get people to do that. As soon as they have money, they want their own space—retirement communities—no noise: isolation. What it does to us! In Scandinavia, where there's basically a birth-to-death kind of social system, suicide among the elderly is incredible! There is no need for retirement communities. We need to live together, integrated generationally. We need to feel *needed* all of our lives.

I'm finding out all these ways people who are marginal survive—living gracefully and simply. Is there a price that can be put on the fact that I can go in any anywhere and *not want anything*? I tell people: every seven years all of your cells are changed in your body. You can begin today to recreate who you are. We can admit we are recovering racists, recovering sexists; just admitting these things gives us the power to change.

Part of what I'm encouraging people to do is to simplify now, while there are no bombs, while there is electricity, while you still have water that you can drink and air that you can breathe. A lot of people say, "Oh, you should be meditating and praying for peace in your heart." I don't know if I'm supposed to have peace in my heart. I don't know if that's my role. I encourage myself to stay anxious. The word *criticas* means *to cut away*, and for me, being a "critica" person is part of being a hag, a crone.

I never think in terms of earning more money, I always think in terms of cutting expenses. I just work and make a couple hundred dollars here and there. My lifestyle is one that doesn't make me spend very much money: I don't have a house, a car, bills. I camp a lot—in people's back-yards, in my tent. I hitchhike or travel with people. I did a drive-away car from Washington, D.C., down to Boca Raton to visit my daughter in

Miami. It cost me $38.00 for gas. That was my sole expense. I took my food with me. I always take my own food.

Clothing is an issue. It's a matter of looking at what you're doing and what you have and saying, "How much do these things possess me?" Those clothes in your closet cause a lot of confusion. You say, "Oh, does this match with this? Oh, what should I wear today?" I'm real creative and I love stuff. If I've got only five pieces of clothing, I can think of a hundred ways to wear them. I'm the same way in the kitchen. There can be three items in that dammed refrigerator and I can come up with twenty ways to fix them. When I take care of food it never goes bad. By having only a few clothes in my backpack I put on what looks best! I always wear my best things! Things that make me feel in my power. If you work with the homeless, and live like they do, you can get clothes out of free boxes. People give it away, so I wear it. I only wear red, white and black because I've simplified my stuff. That way when I look through boxes I don't have to worry about, does it match? Just because you're on the road and poor, doesn't have to mean you're tacky.

All of these little ways add up to our personal power, to our collective power to heal ourselves. I try to use cooking and cleaning as part of my daily meditation. This is a prayer of women all over the world. When I sweep a floor, I am sweeping a floor with literally billions of women. I think this is why the broom is a symbol of women.

I don't inherently have any hatred toward men. I do "Women and Men as Allies" workshops. Yet I feel that women need to concentrate their energy on women and reclaiming Goddess. Men will learn what they need to learn. They need to come to some of their own understanding. It's not my job to teach them. I'm looking for male elders to do that. This male/female thing is going to be an issue for a long time.

There is a spiritual opening going on with me this year. I've been reading about women going through menopause and some of them write the same thing: that it's totally different from what they expected. I think the stage is being set for me to open more in inter-personal relationships through learning conflict resolution. Because I've always just withdrawn from conflict. As an only child I was raised with no conflict. My family was very quiet. They dealt with anger through silence instead of argument.

How do we take back control of our resources? One way is by living below taxable income, a choice I made about 20 years ago. What are the components of a lifestyle of voluntary simplicity? We've been taught not to examine our lives. Many in the culture are crying out for that kind of an examination, that way of looking at what we are doing and the effects of what we are doing on others and ourselves. Ideally, that's part of the role of the grandmothers and of grand parenting—to become the Mother of the World, the Grandparent of the World, to begin to look seven generations into the future.

I believe in recycling. I recycle; every day I practice my power. I believe in vegetarianism, because I know how it impacts the earth when eating meat-centered diet; so every time I eat and cook vegetarian, I am in concert with my beliefs. I am in my power. How do we design a daily lifestyle? What you want to do is practice the power all of the time. This is what I attempt to do—yet I eat dairy products, which is not practicing my power. I am compromising my integrity and I'm totally aware of that. I can name a zillion ways in which I compromise my integrity every day.

They say you begin a journey of a thousand miles with but a single step. When I look down a path that curves around a mountain I can't see what is beyond the curve. The only thing I can do is take those steps and trust. My daily life is practice: practicing being simple, practicing being honest, practicing your prayers, practicing. That is the Tao, that is what I have to do. I need to practice in my everyday life the things I want to see happen. I encourage people to practice now the skills they might need in any situation. Living simply is always going to leave me in a much more flexible position just because of the way I treat my body and myself.

Voluntary simplicity is a way of putting yourself in a space to begin to say: "What is my special gift? How can I manifest—womanifest it in a way that does no harm?" We live in a culture that is harmful. The basis of it is exploitation. It's not a healthy system for us as children of this planet.

We each have a unique thing to offer to this culture. If you look at use as each being perception points of All That Is—each one of us is *unique* and our perceptive ability is based on who we chose to be born to, what body we chose to inhabit, that is a particular perception point. The more clear we are about what that gift is, the more we will manifest it in the universe. What would our lives look like if we lived in a way that did not oppress humans, animals, plants, water, Earth herself, stars—but enhanced them through our prayers, our ceremonies, our gratitude. What might that look like? It's important to posit a vision.

ANCESTRAL DREAMING

Gwendolyn Endicott

On the message machine, once again I listen to the male, computer like voice insist, "I would like to place an order for the book, ANCESTORS. This is the second time I've called." I push "7" to erase the message.

"It's like the frog who came to my back yard before I had a pond," says my friend John. "She sat there and croaked at me and then she went away. That's when I made my pond. I think you're supposed to write this ancestor thing."

In today's mail I received the written order from the persistent bookstore. The book they are sure I have is published by Attic Press and written by someone named Endicott. ANCESTORS it is called.

"Something is going on with the ancestors," I comment to my daughter as we share our recent dreams over the phone, "—since Jeremy's ritual." It is late October at Wanderland, the rainforest where I live near the Oregon coast about a month since my grandson Jeremy's rite of passage. The rains have come and the earth smells sweet with fallen alder leaves. By five in the afternoon, I am shrouded in dusk and drive around the mountain to watch the evening light linger an hour longer over the ocean. We are going down. The falling is coming fast. The lush green is dying back. The earth breathes out cold. We are close to Halloween. In Celtic mythology it is a "between time," a crucial juncture between the seasons. Through the crack in space/time that appears at this juncture, the ancestors come, bringing gifts to their living relation.

Coal Creek, swollen with the fall rains, has swept the gravel bars clean, leaving on one, a small circle of scattered stones—the remains of Jeremy's

30

medicine wheel. Surrounding it is a larger circle of sitting stones, wet in the rain. My mind fills with the memory of the late summer afternoon when we sat here, in the sunshine by the creek's edge, a circle of family and friends, a clan, gathered to support Jeremy's growing from child to man.

Jeremy sits in the South, across from me. In him I see the child I have loved since the moment he was born; in him, I see the child becoming a man. Jeremy is twelve. At times, his father says, he is arrogant, even insolent, and just doesn't care—about anything. Today, Jeremy's face, framed by long black hair, looks very clean—open.

"We are here because we support your growing," I remind Jeremy— "but your root goes deeper still. Many have gone before you who give you the gift of life." Then we named those we remembered, those generations of grandfathers and grandmothers—my own grandfather, who smelled like the earth he farmed and loved; my mother who had the gift of "making"—warm clothes, quilts, apple pies. The foremothers and forefathers of Jeremy were called into the circle; many of their names Jeremy had never before heard. In that moment by the creek at Wanderland, we were a family tree, rooted deeply in the past and blossoming into the future.

Two days after Jeremy's ritual, the ancestral dreaming began. I am drifting between waking and sleeping. My grandfather is standing near me in the room. He is tall and strong. He wears the familiar blue, striped bib-overalls. He is so real I am surprised to see him, yet I know he is a spirit person. As I cry out my greeting, "Granddad, it is so good to see you," and reach out to hug him, my heart flows into his. Coming into waking, I am still filled with the warmth of our embrace.

Perhaps it is because of the new path I named "Grandfather Way" that my grandfather has come to me like this. I ponder the next day. The path leads to an ancient stump, reminder of the giant forest that stood here one hundred years ago. When I first came across the stump, I stood a long time watching as faces and shapes emerged and disappeared in the line and shadow of the wood. It was my grandfather who taught me to "see," to see beyond the surface to the magic, in the rock, in the tree. His presence stayed with me through the days that followed my dream until slowly I began to understand something else. "You stand now for Jeremy where I stood for you," he tells me without the words.

My daughter speaks to me of her dream. She walks toward her grandfather's house. It is small and dark. The curtains are closed as they were when he was dying and she is afraid. What is she doing here, she wonders—at the home of this grandparent who never seemed to understand her, never approved of who she was. Still, she pushes open the sliding glass door and enters. The house fills with light and is tall like a cathedral. Her grandfather stands before her, radiant. Reaching out to her, he gives her a gift. And she feels in that moment his love for her and his support for her path.

My older daughter calls from Seattle and leaves a message on the machine. She has had a dream of her grandmother, she says. And can I call her back? "I am in the kitchen of Grandma and Granddad's house," she says. "I am cooking waffles and I know I am doing it wrong. I am burning them. Smoke fills the house. I know Grandma is going to find me doing it wrong. She comes around the corner into the kitchen. But instead of scolding me, we see each other and our hearts open. All of my guilt and fear and frustration fall away in the love that floods between us."

My daughter goes on to tell me the new adventures of her firstborn, now six months old. Her days are filled with mothering.

A strengthening, a healing, is happening in the roots of our family tree since the rite we created for Jeremy. We wonder at the magic of it and feel its echoes in this place, this remnant of a living rainforest surrounded by clear-cut in the Pacific Coast Range. The roots of my family go six generations into Oregon country. Jeremy's ancestors have been loggers, trappers, hunters, farmers. They have loved Oregon deeply and participated in the destruction of its wilderness. My father lived to see the expanses of forest disappear and the end of the great salmon runs. Jeremy must be taught in schools that such forests and wildlife at one time lived.

"Choose an animal from your medicine wheel," I told Jeremy on the day of his ritual, "and ask what it has to teach you." Alone in the forest,

Jeremy asked Coyote. But it was not Coyote who came. Beyond Jeremy's intending, beyond his choosing, Buffalo appeared. "What you care for will give back to you," the Buffalo said.

The week following the rite of passage, a circle of nine women gathered in retreat at Wanderland on the dark of the moon. After the drumming, the story telling, the dancing, four women stayed awake still longer, to hot tub under the stars. Talking and laughing, enjoying the moment, they told stories of the animals—the elk that run the trails of the forest, the bear who walk the ridge, and the packrat who had moved into the Forest House and nightly collected my ritual items into piles. Then the four women parted each to their tent, to sleep and to dream.

One woman dreamed that she was still in the hot tub, talking and laughing with the others under the stars. Then a large elk walked into the clearing, paused a moment, looked at the woman, and said: "Pardon me, I'd like to speak to you about the elderberries." The next morning she could not remember what it was the Elk wanted her to know.

"Do elk eat elderberries?" she asked me, as my mind raced, remembering the words of the teacher during the plant medicine workshop. "Elderberry is sacred to the elders," she had told us as we walked the upper lane. Ones like these with red berries are poisonous she said quickly moving on to the next plant. "Sacred to the elders," I thought, still looking at the elderberry— "probably because the new shoots sprout right out of the dead wood." I walked numbly behind her, her, words were painful to me. I had been in shock since early that morning when I found the trees along the lower-lane mostly old elderberry, smashed and broken by a neighbor to make way for logging trucks to cross Wanderland. That night, I sat by the creek side, singing and drumming my grief, singing to the elders of the forest, singing for the elderberry trees.

"It's almost Halloween," I tell Jeremy. "What are you going to be?" We are having dinner together in a Portland restaurant. Halloween, I know, is one of his favorite holidays. "I'm just going to be ugly," he replies.

We have spent the dinner hour in animated discussion. Jeremy has, in the last week, experienced his first shamanic journey. His face is full of excitement. Something new and full of wonder has opened in him. "I went to Wanderland," he tells me, "to my circle. The Buffalo came but turned and walked north, upstream. Then a big elk appeared. The elk told me—'you are doing well.'"

"The elk is Grandfather of the place," I reply, looking at Jeremy. He is full of Beauty.

SLEEPING BEAUTY

Shirley Dunn Perry

Sleeping Beauty
sat smiling for the camera
chestnut eyes dancing
curls the same color cascading on bare shoulders
borrowed rhinestone earrings, necklace
reflecting blue and green taffeta dress
hands folded on lap
prince charming cut her communication
with friends, family
blackened her eyes when dinner was late
drank her paycheck, week after week
driving one dark night he ignored her
when she said a truck was coming
head first she flew through the windshield
fifty feet, falling into a ditch
paramedics laid her by the dead boy
who drove the truck
but she woke
face full of glass, broken leg, ribs, right arm
shattered front teeth
the prince blamed her for distracting him
she put herself to sleep, one pill after another
coma is a quiet place

others turn your body
watch your vital signs
feed you through tubes
machines breathe for you
family sit outside
visit, one at a time
three months later
she wakes
without a man's kiss
learns to walk again
builds a home
writes a love poem to herself

MESSAGE FROM THE GODDESS

Maya Levy

The silk sarong around her naked flesh felt cool, like rain. Silk she'd dyed, for other women. Wealthy women. She never wore her silks herself. They were much too grand. She only sold her work in galleries and shops. Why had this piece never sold? The crepe de chine was 55 inches wide, an unusual find. The blues, roses, mauves and blacks blended together like leopards sleeping in the shade. Oh well. Since she no longer worked with silk, this one had been tucked away in a drawer, waiting for what, she didn't know.

She'd never worn a sarong before. Sarongs were for other women in tropical resorts, TV commercials, on private yachts. Thin, glamorous, sexy women. Even when she was young, she'd never seen herself as thin, lovely, and sexy. She marveled. Here she was, at her age, tying this luscious piece of beauty around her breasts, preparing to meet her lover. She giggled. The woman reflected in the mirror was beautiful. Not thin. Not young. She raised her arms over her head, and let her body sway. Her shoulder slowly moved forward. She wiggled her hips. Beautiful. Definitely sexy.

There'd been no man for her since her husband died eight years before. So long. Too long. She'd never been without a boyfriend, husband, lover, since third grade when the new boy in class gave her a gold ring that turned her finger green.

So many men. Her first husband, handsome in a leading man sort of way, and a good provider, was an abysmal lover. She thought he'd improve with age, but she was wrong. One day, after her hysterectomy, she realized she could now sleep with anyone she wanted to. Pregnancy was no longer in her reality.

That trip to the Bahamas, with a group of friends, she'd had her first affair. Then another, and another and another. Her sexuality opened wide, like flower petals to the warming sun. Each man taught her new and deeper pleasure. The university professor, so obsessed with aberrant sexual practices of strange tribes on foreign soil. The pro football player, much younger than she, who admired her brain. The Transylvanian novelist who tried to lure her into a menage a'trois with his English fiancé. The executive, who put her up in fancy hotels in the city. The ex-husband of her best friend.

Then she met him. He came into her life before she was divorced. As an acquaintance. An oddity. An artist. It was only after she'd left home that he became her lover. When she'd forsaken husband, children, job, everything she'd ever known to search for her own creativity, her own artistry. When he'd parted from the woman he was with.

Their passion knew no bounds. Swimming in the lake or in their favorite stream, he'd enter her, like water. Fill her up till she'd nearly drown in pleasure. They'd make love all night long, on a pallet on his studio floor, their sweat-wet bodies sliding over each other like waterfalls slipping over soft river stones. He painted pictures for her, of trees, earth, and sky. She wrote poems for him of leprechauns and untamed cats that lived forever.

He went back to the woman he'd left.

She wept bitter tears. Bitter, bitter tears.

She went on. To another man. A good man. A kind man. A brilliant man. A sensual man who loved her strongly. She came to love him beyond measure. They married. She knew at last true love. Unconditional love. Faithful love. The idea of being with another man never even entered her head. He died too soon. She mourned as if part of her had died because it had. The best part.

She realized that it had been best that her lover had left her. The ten years she had with her husband were so rich, so full of life, love, passion, pain...she would never trade them. Not for all the stars in the sky. She grieved so when he died. She feared her tears would flood the world, they seemed so unending. The idea of being with another man was unthinkable. Who could compare. No one. Through the years, of hardship and pain, she came to wonder if she would ever feel alive again. She feared her heart must surely have turned to brittle stone.

Then, only a few weeks ago as summer solstice came and passed, her mourning fell away like a dark veil drifting away. And she felt her femaleness. She wanted someone now. To feel his maleness. And so she prayed to the Goddess to send her a man. A lover. She wrote it down on bits of colored paper and scattered them on her altar, before Venus, Isis and Inanna, who knew about such things.

Never in her wildest dreams did she imagine it would be him. She was sitting in bed one morning, working, when he called that late summer morning.

She hung up, feeling very strange. She could hardly believe it was true. He was back in her life after eighteen years. Why was he calling, after all this time? She'd seen him off and on throughout the years, but hardly said hello. She didn't want to say anything to him; he'd hurt her so. Then she remembered. He'd called one afternoon, long ago, when she and her husband were making love. He didn't know she'd married. She knew he had. That things did not go well. His wife was a volatile woman, given to violent ways. Someone once filed for divorce, she'd seen in the paper. She knew his life had never been happy.

They met for coffee. When he walked up, she felt that old familiar flutter in her stomach. He was still beautiful to her. He'd gained weight, as had she. His beard was white, as was what little hair still curled around his ears. But he had those smiling eyes. And gentle ways. They talked of this and that. Of her career. His life. He had grandchildren. She had none, but hoped. He said his marriage had never been good.

Now, a week later, here she was standing before her mirror, adorning herself in precious silk, letting him back into her life. This was who Goddess sent. What strange karma was winding through her life, and his, she didn't know. All she could do was follow the golden threads spinning around them, like Ariadne's thread leading deep into the Minoan maze.

Her body had changed. Would he mind the extra pounds around her middle? And her arms. The lines across her face. Her straight hair was still blonde, a gift from the genie in the bottle. And it was long, falling past her shoulders to spread wide, like Saharan sand. She never liked her straight hair when she was young, but now she loved it.

Would her body even remember how? It'd been so long. Could she even do it? Could he?

They sat together on the sofa, looking at each other's faces. Smiling. Touching. He told he she was beautiful. Gorgeous was what he really said. She told him of her fears. He said he was nervous too.

She took away his clothes, and wrapped him in a piece of silk she'd painted, of Medusa, with jeweled serpents holding up the sky. He wanted to see her naked, but she was shy. And so they kissed, beneath the covers of her bed. It was incredibly soft she moaned. She touched his face, his snow-white beard. Loved his baldhead with her hands. His hands lost themselves in her body and all the silk. They looked deep into each other's eyes, and smiled.

They were on each other like two wild things, tearing through a curtain of years and an avalanche of desire. He ripped away the silk and found her breast, her stomach, and her thighs. She wrapped her body around him every way she could, trying to feel every inch of him. They called each other's names, over and again. He made his way into her. Nothing had ever felt so warm. So pure. He moved deep and wide, into her softness. And her body remembered.

They were done too soon. Finished. Spent. Their passion was so great it consumed them. Overwhelmed them. Covered them with glory. She felt like a newborn babe, seeing the world for the very first time. Everything glowed and danced, alive with power.

The second time he came to her, they never left the sofa. He yanked her clothes away and filled her up like wild wind, blowing. All their years of longing, years of wanting roared away, like dust.

He came to her again. They lay cocooned together upon the moonlit grass outside, looking up. She wanted him to go. Leave. No. To escape this whirling tide of them before it sucked her away and she was lost. He wrapped himself around her. She held him fiercely, never wanting him to leave. He kissed her. She caught the scent of him. Earthy. Clay. And she was gone, lost in the smell of him. The savage soil of him.

Their lovemaking that night lasted for hours upon her feather bed. They touched, gently, softly feeling all the tiny places of each other. She traced the contours of his face with her fingers. Found the hollows of his ears, elbows, and eyes. Touched him with her toes. Felt the outline of his lips with hers. He pressed his strong hands into her back and stroked her hips, kissing her hair, his eyes and hands feasting on her soft white skin.

They were travelers together, learning a brave new world. He was inside her now, rubbing. Touching her quietly. Peacefully. Still, like silence. All her body felt was... awe. Like being touched by God. He felt it too. "This is divine," he said. "Divine." She knew that it was true. And then they were gone. Lost in the worlds of each other. They found themselves walking upon the sky. Wandering. In and out of mystery. Their bodies opened into wonderment. They pounded wide the gates of heaven and fell, into the arms of God.

The weeks went by. He made drawings of them naked together, erotic, poetic. She wrote psalms to him. A sex goddess at her age? How wonderful. How great. To be so adored. To know her power, which she'd never really thought about, when she was young.

Her body remembered, from the dawn of time, from every woman she'd ever been, every woman making love to every man. She found new ways to love, moving against him with all her strength and lust. Testing her power. Expanding it, like a jungle cat on lava rocks, stretching. Challenging him. Teasing him. Loving him like a courtesan. Like a saint.

How she loved it. As did he. She was a feral thing, running free through the forests of his being. He threw himself into the river of her soul, to float upon the waves lapping at the borders of her dreams. He filled her up like wolf songs fill the night. She followed him where neither one had been before. She led him into places high like pyramids. Into places deep, like ancient caves.

Aphrodite was alive within her, moving her beyond the limits of human sexuality. Lifting them, holding them aloft on some jubilant fountain flowing from the center of the earth. Moving them to hallowed ground where they were Sacred Female, Sacred Male. His bed was heaven on earth and he was God, she Goddess.

He was whom the Goddess sent. Yet, deep in her most secret hidden place where no one was allowed, she knew. Whatever karma was weaving its way through their lives would never be complete, in this lifetime. He yearned to grow, as an artist, as a man, a spiritual self. But he would not, could not break free from his wife, the tormented life he wanted so to flee. This affair was not forever. Only for a while. She hoped she brought him beauty, joy, life. Hope. He gave her back her body, her sexuality. Her woman's heart. They would ever be bound together, with silken strands of love and longing. But they would never be together. One day they would part. They would cry, and rejoice, and go on. She, with her life, her work. Her art. There would be another man for her, whom she would love in ways new and strange and grand. Because he had come into her life to give her back herself.

But till that day, she would love him best she could. With all of her body. That was what she had to give. She knew now, what she'd never really felt till now when she was old. She had to be old; it seemed, to finally get it. Being a sex goddess, at this older time of her life, well, it was Divine. Sacred. Blessed. This was the gift she brought. The message from the Goddess. To feel, in every dot, every tiny speck of her, to truly know at last, that she was Holy. That she was Goddess too.

In The Beginning, We Were Daughters

"Generations of women have sacrificed their lives to become their mothers. But we do not have that luxury anymore. The world has changed too much to let us have the lives our mothers had. And we can no longer afford the guilt we feel at *not* being our mothers. We cannot afford *any* guilt that pulls us back to the past. We have to grow up, whether we want to or not. We have to stop blaming men and mothers and seize every second of our lives with passion. We can no longer afford to waste our creativity. We cannot afford spiritual laziness."

Erica Jong

WE, THE GIRL CHILDREN OF THE TRIBE, FIND OUR OWN

Lynne Namka (author credit)

"There is an Emergent Evolution taking place."

Alice Bailey

How do we women ever find out who we are? We have spent our formative years living with that most imposing, all life-giving mother. The single most significant figure in a woman's life is her mother. The fury and weakness as well as the strength of feminine power of the female ancestral line are passed down to us through our mothers.

We sort and sift through out our lives taking what is best for us and hopefully letting the rest go. We grapple with rage against her, and we love and honor our mother. We fight the conflict of the opposing needs for connection with our mothers and union and fierce independence. We start in total symbiosis with the mother and spend countless years moving apart and coming back to her. Throughout life we struggle to become the best parts of our mother and let go of her negative qualities. In later years, if we have successfully addressed this endless task, we have the chance for happiness.

The lengths that we go to avoid our mother's destiny are endless. Many young girls grow up vowing, "I will not be the type of mother/woman/wife/ that my mother was." As children we were determined to be different: to be more loving, less critical, less needy than our mothers. Often we repress and deny those dark parts, which were modeled for us. We rail and scream, "I will not be my mother" while discouraged to find that we engage in similar behaviors.

We were well schooled in the energetic patterns that made up our mothers. At times it seems as if there is no escape. Our relationship with our mother as well as her relationship with our father is played out again across our decades. Embarrassed, we see the patterns of the family being performed with ourselves in the starring role as we move in and out of relationships. We hear our mother's voice coming out of our mouth; we watch her rules pop up in us when least expected. We project our mother's worst faults onto others replaying those old family scripts. Others, especially men, project their mother's stuff onto us and we project ours right back on them.

Despite good intentions and hard work, we find remnants of our mothers in us—in our voice patterns, habits, belief systems and unconscious choices. Carl Jung told us that what we do not make conscious, we draw back to us as fate. Jung described how children are taught to repress certain parts of their personality to fit in and conform to social mores. The more the girl child conforms, the more she gives up of herself until she is but a remnant of her original self. Jung describes role reversal as a task of the second half of life where we can learn to balance and integrate those parts of ourself that were squelched by our mother or where we over identified with her darker nature. What we have not learned to do well in the first part of our life can be made a conscious choice to learn in the second half. Adding the complement to our over practiced behaviors in the second half of life provides the opportunity to be a well-rounded individual.

As older women, one of our most sacred tasks is to reclaim those parts of ourselves that were denied. The mother work must be done if we are to find happiness in being who we are. The myths of being women in relationships to others must be examined. It is in working the darkest mother stuff that we discover who we are. As we reach our final years, with great discernment, we come into our own and find our own identity.

So wrap your shawls around those shoulders, which have been weighed down with the burdens of being born and raised female in this world. Listen with your heart to release those burdens you have carried with you since childhood. Invite the story spirits in to assist you in letting go of that which no longer fits you. Square your shoulders and feel your resolve as you lean forward to hear the wisdom of those whose journey has been similar to your own. Lean forward and sharpen your breath as the stories begin...

MY MOTHER TAUGHT ME HOW TO PRAY

Geri Gilbert

You wore black shoes with laces,
solid purple on Sunday
and flour-smudged aprons
over soft clinging dresses.
You baked, first sifting bugs
from flour: bread, biscuits
and pie made from lard
stretching dough thin
with a wooden pin squeaking.
On Saturday you scrubbed
floors and sometimes us
with vengeance
washed my mouth with soap
at least once when I lied.
Whether we listened or not
you talked—a handkerchief
doing its white linen best
to hide whispers in church.
You cried when I hurt
clasping me close to flesh
smelling warm rose-lavender,
blowing out sadness
into that lace-edged linen

pocketed between breasts.
When you took off your apron
powdered your nose
and sat at the piano to sing
Nearer My God to Thee,
our yearning was me.
A lace-edged linen
hangs on my bathroom wall
blue shadow of a form
crossing a bridge
painfully, slowly,
Mt. Fiji in the distance.

WOMEN IN PARADOX

Jane Evans

I will not be my grandmother
Blind, senile, calling out for her dead child of forty years,
Raiser of daughters whose anger caused them to fall in and out
    with each other.
My programming was to take care of the needy and helpless.
For who will care for the sick and ill, if not me?
Blind to my own needs, I have fulfilled the caretaking role.
I will not be this grandmother.
Who then will I be, if not my grandmother?

I will not be my other grandmother.
Fearful, martyr, enabler of men in their weakness.
Doing for all and depressed that all leave her.
My programming was to take care of men.
For who will take care of the unfaithful man, if not me?
Frightened of being alone, I have stayed in despair, calling it love.
I will not be this other grandmother.
Who then will I be, if not my other grandmother?

I will not be my mother.
Sick and tired of being sick and tired.
Benevolent dictator lying on the couch,
Demanding the absent man be present.

My programming was to chase those who withdrew.

For who will run after men who are unavailable, if not me?

Sick and tired, I have sought those who defend themselves against
my love.

I will not be this mother.

Who then will I be, if not my mother?

Who then will I be if I repudiate these women's values and
lifestyles?

These women who have shaped my attitudes, behaviors and style
of a life.

They live within me still despite many degrees, groups and thera-
pies—

Dependency, martyrdom, illness and fear of madness

Have haunted me relentlessly across the course of my time.

Genetic memories, images of who I have been swim before me.

The murderous savage caught in a thirst for blood and a frenzy of
lust.

The heavyset nun, wimpled and weary, content with my simple
laboring,

The teller of tales, weaving my spell in the light of the flickering
campfire.

The tribesman, dancing wildly to the rhythm of ancient drums,

The medicine woman, gathering my herbs, sharing my craft with
those who follow

The dark mother, Kali, all life giving and consuming,

All of these, both of the dark and light,

These I am and more, much more.

I use their dark energy to embrace the past,

Knowing who I have been is only a forerunner of who I am
becoming.

Furiously I run forward seeking new images.
Who then will I be if not them?
Who then shall I be?

Now, at this age, I refuse the energetic patterns of my women
    ancestors
Fiercely, I seek richer archetypes for my definition of woman.
Secretly, I study older women in restaurants, libraries and art gal-
    leries
Taking what I like from each, tossing out old scripts, rewriting old
    programs
Gathering images of other women I have longed to know, to
    become...
The gutsy, sensual, toothless woman laughing in the soup kitchen
    line.
The cheerful, caring countenance of the clerk in an occult book-
    store.
The frail, yet firm of step, clarity of the artist, lover of life at age 90.
The strident, angry, determination of the activist fighting for
    social justice.
The high energy, enthusiasm and vitality of my teacher, challeng-
    ing me to be whole.
The gentle, loving energy of the older friends accepting me,
    imperfect as I am.
Hungrily, I take from snatches of courage and valor from each,
Piecing together my new patchwork of woman of wisdom,
A postmenopausal process of knowing who I am and who I am not.
The bleeding stopping, the fierceness of Truth emerging.
Now I no longer need to define myself through others,
I no longer actively seek older role models,
Slowly I grow and accept the uniqueness that is me.

Women, older women, come into my consciousness—
Women, finding strength in being vulnerable,
Women, standing straight and tall, supporting others,
Women, shedding their defenses to find safety,
Women, becoming crazy to discover sanity,
Women, walking straight into their own pain, to move through it,
Women, denying the external male god to find holiness within,
Women, coming together in groups to discover their individuality,
Women, making new and different choices than those who came
    before.

Women, older women stepping forward to claim identity and
    integrity.
Women who gleefully reject negative models and stereotypes,
Saying, "I am not this. I throw out the old to welcome in the new."
Women, today's women, strong-minded women,
Most marvelous women, bonding together.
Sharing their stories, rewriting their lives to create a peaceful
    world.
We fiercely forge ourselves out of new steel,
A magnificent sculpture of feminine fulfillment in the making.
We change the meaning of what it means to be a woman.
We do it for those women ancestors, who came before,
As well as for ourselves, for our children and those who are yet to be.
We are the new women, the new, improved model.
Women in paradox, taking a new heritage.

MOTHERS

Joyce A. Kovelman

The Gathering of Grandmothers gave me cause to think about my own mother. I recalled that when I wished her, "Happy Birthday," she didn't know how old she was. When I replied that she was now 89 years old, she smiled and shyly said, "Ooh, that much." She has taught me that "old" is not a dirty word. Rather it is the privilege of a life well lived. And, I remembered the day my friend's mother told me that she was having "a bad memory day." Bravely, this Grandmother acknowledged her limits, and then continued on her way. All of these women have endowed me with inspiration and the understanding that Aging bestows its own special gifts.

I have just returned from a rare visit to my 79-year-old mother. She grows more fragile every time I see her. I grow aware that I am losing a part of her daily. She is suffering from "acute old age." Mom has lived to see her children and grandchildren grow; now she is determined to hold her first great-grandchild before she dies.

After my last visit, I thought about mothers. I became aware of the great variation of motherhood all about me. There are good mothers and bad mothers, biological mothers, adopted mothers, surrogate mothers, expectant mothers, foster mothers and stepmothers. There are also single mothers, working mothers, welfare mothers, Mother Goose, Mommie, Dearest, Mother Earth and Mother Nature to contend with. I recognize grandmothers, great grandmothers, Mother-in-laws, the Queen Mother and Mother Superior, as well. The diversity is endless.

Mothers are important; they nurture, birth and sustain all humanity. Mothers are the honored caretakers of life. It is a truly awesome responsibility. All of humankind is born of Woman. Without Mothers, we could not be.

But, humankind shows a disdain and disrespect for Mothers. We forget to call or visit them, we argue and tell them how much smarter we are, we refuse to listen to their stories or wishes, and we often make jokes about our Mothers. Mothers are blamed for all of humankind's failings, individually and collectively. Rather than acknowledge our Mother's wisdom, intuition and caring, we shamefully turn away. Even Mother Earth is experiencing the wrath and waste of humanity, as we desecrate our land, water and sky. Humanity is destroying its planetary home.

Why is it so hard to love our Mothers? Why do we choose to share anger instead of appreciation? Why do we blame them for all our problems? What would happen if we were to honor our Mothers all year long, rather than just one day a year?

Then I started to think about my own motherhood. I felt sad. The early warning signs were already there. My children were absorbed in their own lives and problems; they didn't have enough time to hear about mine. I wondered if it was possible to change the attitudes of society and especially my own family's thinking about Mother. I yearned for warmth, connection and relationship. I wanted to be respected for a life well lived, for love and compassion; I do not want to be considered an "old fool" when I am old and gray. No wonder women are afraid to grow up and age.

My thoughts turn to life and to its value and its purpose. I grew aware that humankind must again reaffirm the sacredness of all existence. Only a species who recognizes and honors each and every life, will know how to respect and treat its Mothers. Let us begin the task of healing Mother Earth. As we heal our planetary home, we also heal our relationships, families, communities and society. We will become the Mothers who will birth a sacred, new World.

I Am My Mother

Anonymous

I am my mother.

She reaches out and touches me through the years and through the great gulf of life and death that separates us. She laughs with me and nudges my conscience, even yet. I feel her love like a blanket. I see her smile and remember the very smell of her. I cherish our private secrets and still keep them quietly locked away even though she's so long gone now.

What did she give me? Life, love, information, security, self-confidence, food, clothes, joy, heartaches, lumps and independence. But more that, she gave me herself. Part of me is her. The way I hold my head is her. The way I squirrel away money is her. The way I feel about other people is her. The anger that sometimes surfaces through my cool is hers. The special feeling I have about myself is her. My ability to give without asking for return investment is hers, and my dread of cleaning out the refrigerator is her dread.

Love is eternal. Her love for me has become a part of my love for my children even though they never knew her in life. She was wrong some-times. She messed up my life sometimes. She liked the wrong boys, dragged me to the wrong places and accused me of things I did not do. She gave my sister things I wanted. She ran off to the movies without me. She always favored my brother. She fussed at my father way too much.

Why in the world do I love her? Along with the mystery of developing bones in the womb is a greater mystery—the developing spirit. Through some part of God's genius, mothers give their children not only bones, blood and breath but also a part of their soul. I am not only me. I am her.

Even when she was wrong, I somehow knew she loved me. Even when I hated her, I know I loved her. Inside of me is a piece of her soul and we are linked together for eternity for better or worse.

She's been gone a long time. I see her eyes in my daughter. I hear her laughter from the throat of my son. I feel her terror in a phone call from my daughter late at night. Her outspokenness is screamed at by a child in distress. Her forgiveness encircles me as I forgive. Her thoughtfulness arrives in a bouquet from a grown child. Her impulsiveness scares me witless in the daring of my granddaughter. She lives. I live. We are eternal.

On Becoming a Loose Woman

Movement is life. Movement is my medicine. It is the mechanism for surrender. I surrender to movement, I surrender to what is. I am not just talking about movement of the body, but movement of the entire psyche. Movement of the heart; movement of the mind…Indeed, if you put the psyche in motion it will heal itself; we all have that power. The fastest way to still the mind is to move the body. The temple of the familiar is the mind. The body is the mind it is the heart. If I kick you in the shin you will feel it; it will hurt. Then it will immediately start to heal itself. This indicates to me that both your heart and your mind are in your shin. It's all one…

That is why movement is our medicine because it is very direct.

Gabrille Roth

SEEKING THE FLUID SELF

Lynne Namka (author credit)

"Therefore, find your own way, open your treasure house,
invent your own answer to the chaos.
And please remember when you get there, there isn't any there there."

Gertrude Stein

Throughout our lives we women alternately play the transformational game of gain and loss. We gain things only to lose them; this theme of inevitable loss prepares us for the final and greatest task...death. In youth we give credence to beauty, health, security, material goods and personal gain. Strength, agility, speed, physical beauty are the outer trappings of the human personality, which can fade with time. Likewise friends, loved ones and our lofty positions are of a temporary nature.

All is transitory in life. save that which is of the Spirit. Loss can be sobering. It sets us back on our heels—asking us to take stock. But as Virginia Satir said, "Humans are made to integrate loss. Each loss makes another gain," It is through acceptance of losing things, those unessential parts of our life, that we become loose. With grace and understanding, loss can help us to become looser. Loss can help us find a more fluid version of ourselves.

The rigidity of youth, which seeks absolute truth, seeing things in an either/or framework of thinking, gives way. As we age, the black and white way of viewing the world gives way to a gradual release from egocentric clinging. Maturity adapts the either/or philosophy of viewing things to finding a place of acceptance. Life's lessons teach flexibility and tolerance of conflicting ideas. Balance is found in the center. This is fluidity as spoken by the willow, which bends and sways with the storms and rains of life. Women weather their personal storms through deep introspection, acceptance and graceful movement. After a period of chaos, a self-defined woman returns to the center of her calm.

The older years are about bringing balance to one's life. The self-seeking indulgence of youth can be balanced with a generous spirit in the later years. This is the process of balancing the needs of the individual with altruistic concerns for others in society. For some women, the later years become a time to move from the self-involved perspective of obtaining material goods to developing humanistic endeavors. Research shows that as people mature, altruistic behavior increases. A generosity of heart and spirit indicates good mental health and a willingness to let go of unnecessary attachments.

Women, who have given up their individuality to meet the needs of others, now can reclaim their identity. The second half of life can be a time for giving up some of the worldly pursuits and finding a form of living that allows time for doing inner work. Balance. A woman's life is balanced by subtracting what there is too much of and adding what is lacking.

At midlife, if we have not done so already, we are prompted to develop our masculine side. Goal-directed and action-oriented behavior, suppressed by early parental programming and societal pressure, may begin to break through. For good mental health, positive masculine attributes must be brought forth to complement the feminine side. The urge to express oneself through assertiveness and movement emerges from the unconscious mind as we seek the balance of energies. The merging of the masculine and feminine energies within is one of the great tasks of the second half of life.

Self-exploration becomes a daily task for those serious about the process of growth as we march down the years. The breakthrough of discovery is finding the inner treasure of introspection, enjoyment of leisure time and self-reformation. It is the breaking down of old structures that no longer fit and finding a new supple aspect of ourselves. We can turn to our symbol-laden unconscious to help deal with the resignation and despair that loss brings.

Spiritual transcendence is transforming the rigid ego attachments into acceptance of self and others. This is one of the major tasks in later life. Jung's work described this process of being one of Enlightenment where the ego and the self become integrated. Wisdom gained through out the lifetime helps transform losses and suffering through reflection and introspection.

Integrity is the ability to accept one's past choices and actions and go forth and act in accordance with one's deepest values from within. This self-honesty comes from a well-formed conscience which insists on living up to firm standards and values. Integrity insists on affirmation for self and others alike. If integrity in the later years is not found, the individual falls into inevitable pride, bitterness and despair about what has not been accomplished in one's lifetime. Research shows that successful older peo-ple have developed a problem-solving style of drawing from past experi-ence to tackle new challenges. Healthy elders view the past as worthwhile life lessons from which they have learned and moved on. They are willing to let go of the irrational fads and ideas prescribed by the culture and see things realistically from inner knowing.

By letting go of the hype and drama of the world, we learn to celebrate more fully who we are. Older women no longer need to be caught up in the idealistic righting of wrongs or excesses of serving others to the exclu-sion of our own selves as a way of justifying our existence. We learn what is called process living—to really be present in the moment instead of liv-ing from a role or behind a mask. Staying presents requires that we become more aware of our pain, our joys and the big and small rites of passage that dot our lives. We sit with our emotions and process them to glean what wisdom we can. Process living asks us to focus on that which is really important. And then risk going into the unknown! As Bernice

Reagon, curator and historian of the National Museum of History, said, "Once you get to menopause, you're going to fly!"

In the elder years we can move more and more into the simplicities. That which is true and beautiful becomes even more so—the innocent smile of a child, the first violet after the winter, the cobalt blue of the teapot, a Palo Verde tree glistening with dew drops, the holiness within our soul. We can return home to our innocence that we gave up so many years ago as small children.

Small fruits shine when we learn to just be in the process of becoming who we are. In process living, we take responsibility for our thoughts, words and actions. We can insist on being brutally honest with ourselves. We understand release and movement. With a limited amount of time left to be here on this earth, we begin to refuse to take crap from others or from ourselves. We learn to act as if what we choose makes a difference because it does. In making our choices from the simplicity of the Wise Old Woman part of ourselves, we honor our process of growing into our true selves.

So prepare yourself now for the storytelling. Once again, call in the story spirits—call them to come directly to your fears born of "But what will other people think?" Prepare for the shifting of the inflexible, the loosening of old rigidities whose culturized bonds have held you tight. Invite the stories in, now gather around and let us hear...

WISE WOMEN ON CHANGE

This divine discontent is born of the spirit. It is the will toward freedom and life, not the discount of the desirous ego that seeks its own aggrandizement, or the discontent of the child who clamors for small satisfactions. It is the discontent that will not let man rest until he has found the creative meaning of his own individual life. For true creativity is not concerned with the ego, but with the Self.

Frances G. Wickes

Odd how the creative power at once brings the whole universe to order.

Virginia Woolf

When I came to understand that there are mythic patterns in all our lives, I knew that all of us, often unbeknownst to ourselves, are engaged in a drama of soul which we were told was reserved for gods, heroes and saints.

Deena Metzger

The human mind is like a piñata; when it breaks open, there's lots of surprises inside. Once you get the piñata experience, you see that losing your mind can be a peak experience.

Trudy, Lily Tomlin's bag lady character

Every time things get dull, I ratchet my life up a bit. Change, constant change, is my middle name.

Jane Evans

The word "attract" means to "to draw." You are a magnetic field of mental influence…What you attract depends upon than on which you dwell.

Catherine Ponder

I sweat my prayers. Prayer is silence. Prayer isn't a lot of words; it's not a repetition of a lot of clever words; it's not begging somebody else to do something about your life. It is really getting down to the bone. We are mysterious, unpredictable and something that will never be truly understood. So, we may as well step back and be awed.

Gabrille Roth

I'm learning how to become a loose woman.

June Keen

And the day came when the risk to remain tight in a bud was more painful than the risk it took to blossom.

Anais Nin

WHAT I DID ON MY SUMMER VACATION

Nana Gaia

As my 50th birthday approached, I was challenged to figure out just how I wanted to celebrate this special occasion. The previous year I had filled my house with wonderful friends, family, a live band, and all the trimmings. How was I to top that? I got to thinking about various ways I had honored others I love in my life, and I realized that often I had taken the time and trouble to go away on a vacation with just that person. I was amazed to discover that I had never spent a week alone, by myself. I had married and had my first child at 19 years old, and now at 49 my last child was still with me! I was appalled to think that I had never cared enough about myself to take the time and trouble to create special time and space for my very own self. Yes, yes, yes! It seemed like the perfect thing to do. I would plan a weeks' vacation from my job as a home health nurse and go off somewhere with only myself as company.

The next challenge was to figure out where I wanted to do such a thing. The home of my soul is virgin nature, so my first thought was to find a site somewhere in the wilderness areas around my home in Eugene, Oregon. The other important consideration was privacy. That posed a bit of a problem; for I had no way of limiting access to any site I chose, if I were in public use lands. After a little consideration, I thought of some forestland that I "owned" cooperatively with a group of people. In 1968 1 had left the dominant paradigm and sought an alternative lifestyle in the forests of Oregon. The family we had created still held onto the property where we had lived communally in the 60's. Each year we had returned for a family reunion, so I had maintained a fond connection with this land.

Yes! I could surely find a safe, secure spot on this land to cloister myself for a week before my 50th birthday.

I was truly excited to fulfill my plans and bought myself a small 14-foot tepee in honor of the occasion. I went down to the land and roamed all over, looking for an area new to me, unimpregnated with old memories. I found the perfect site, close to a tiny stream, and far away from the log lodge and other dwellings we had built some 22 years before. A few weekends before my birthday, my dog, a friend and I went down to the space, leveled the site, put up the tepee poles, and generally got the feel of the land. Then we wrapped up my gear in a tarp, stashed it beneath a grove of trees, and covered it all with leaves. Then, back to Eugene to gather last minute supplies, fulfill my work commitment and prepare for my first ever week by myself!

My excitement grew as the days passed. I intended that this week be sweet and simple. I chose to do a modified fast of brown rice and fluids, and of course my faithful coffee! I didn't want to be distracted by outside influences, so I did not bring many books just my *I Ching*, an empty journal, and at the last moment, a book lent to me by a friend. I hoped to fulfill a longstanding desire to "write a book" by filling up this empty journal with all the events, ramblings and reflections of this week by myself I bought a new set of colored pens, and decided that the only rule about the book was that there would be no rules at all! I could fill up the empty pages with whatever I wanted, whenever I wanted, however I wanted!

Little by little, step by step, each little detail fell into place and finally the day arrived to leave for the land. I asked my friend to drive me down to the land and then take my car back to Eugene, so that my campsite would be less noticeable and so that I would not have the option to change my mind and leave before the week was up. He was to return one week later to help me break my fast of solitude and help me celebrate my birthday.

The two-hour drive was sweet and effortless. When we arrived I went over to retrieve the stashed items, only to find that everything was gone, stolen! No machete! No hatchet! No propane stove nor fuel! No mattress!

No tarp! No privacy, for whoever stole the items knew the site and that someone would be arriving soon. As I listened to the crack of the rifles of the hunters in the hills nearby, a shiver of fear passed through me. I took a deep breath and went inside. What was my intent? What had I expected? It was not long before a strong sense of serenity and purpose returned. I felt confident of my goal, and secure that my pure heart and my big dog would see me through.

My friend wandered off to see what he could find, and returned with a foam pad and a tarp. The poles had been left as they were standing and we had taken the canvas for the tipi with us, so my shelter was intact. I had brought a small axe and a bow saw with me and I had my cooking pots, so I felt that I had all that I needed for my week. The stream had dried up, so that meant I had to walk about a mile for bathing in the creek, but that was no problem. We had brought plenty of drinking water. All was well. With a tender hug and kiss, my friend drove off with the car and I was left alone, with my dog, my hopes and fears, my dreams and visions,

Each day filled itself to full, having to find and haul enough wood to enable me to make a fire every time I wanted a little hot water. I found a huge stash of discarded madrone, left as garbage by some loggers, but a premium treasure for me and my tepee. The black madrone burns hot and smoke free, and the little dried twigs, her fingernails, are perfect for kindling. Soon a routine was established of rising at first light, starting the fire, tai chi and yoga for my aging and aching body, meditation in the golden rising sun, and journaling after my meditation and whenever I felt like it.

After my morning meal, it was off to the madrone stash to haul down some limbs, bow saw the wood into usable pieces, stack it in the tepee, and gather enough fingernails to start the precious flame. By then it was time for something to eat, and then off to bathe in the cold stream in the heat of the day. I'd hang out by the water till the cool of the afternoon so that the walk back to my campsite was comfortable, and so that I wouldn't work up another sweat to spoil my cooling, cleansing bath. By then it was time to make another fire for my evening meal, and to enjoy the sweet companionship and heat of the flames, and the comfort of its light. Soon I was sleeping soundly on my pad on the ground, tired after my full day of "chop wood and carry water."

It was a wonderful and pivotal time in my life, my first week of solitude before my 50th birthday. I came to see that I really enjoyed my own company. It was a monastic life style, filling my day with my own personal, eclectic spiritual practice, and the activities necessary for survival. This simple life felt infinitely familiar and comfortable. The journal filled itself effortlessly, and was like a companion. My inner beloved and my faithful attentive dog were company enough.

By the time the week was up, I had created for myself my own morning practice. I had come to realize how much I missed the constancy of my former practice, which I had learned from years of following my guru. This time, the content and sequence of the form came from within myself. It filled my own mandates and criteria. I was pleasing no one outside myself. I was happy, I was content, and I was fulfilled in my present practice. I also came in touch with my longing for a circle of women. I promised myself that when I returned to Eugene, I would invite some of my women friends over to see about starting a moon circle. I had dreams and hopes and plans for the future.

Sooner than expected my birthday arrived, and with it my long time friends came to help me break my modified fast of food and solitude with their precious love, delicious treats and chocolate delights.

Now it is five and a half years later. The moon circle of women continues to meet each month. It has been a profound influence on all its co-creators, empowering and enriching each one of us. My daily practice also continues, as I have been faithful to pray, stretch, meditate and journal every morning since those first days, now so long ago. This devotion to my own process and my own personal eclectic, spiritual practice has been an immeasurable source of strength, comfort and guidance in my life. In fact, the years since that first week alone in the forest have been the best years of my life. I know that more, so much more, is yet to come.

WISE WOMEN ON ATTACHMENTS

It is a gift to give someone your hand, but not your back.

Virginia Satir

We must all be willing to outgrow what no longer fits.

Gail Sheely

Knowledge of the Self consists not at all of the conclusions formed in autoerotic introspection, but of coming to terms with inner forces, which we do not invent but discover, in a moving experience. So it is through conscious relatedness with a fellow man that he may realize the Self. And with a reciprocal action the Self alone makes real relatedness possible.

Eleanor Bertine

The feminine principle is necessary for the healing of addictions.

Marion Woodman

The ability to recognize the nature of this crisis, to express the fears, confusion, regrets and bitterness, will allow the individual woman to come into a new life as the process of mourning for the end of youth gives way to the re-emergence of hope. Life comes, for out of the end of the old, something new emerges—perhaps unbidden. Risking, trusting the future, finding hope that new forms of personal self-understanding and worth will emerge are qualities that are given, discovered. The new identity, the new strength, the new direction that can emerge for a woman as life changes comes not so much from conscious planning but from parts of the self hidden and unexpressed for many years.

Being very rich, so far is as I am concerned, is about having a margin. The margin is being able to give.

May Sarton

The shock of painful experiences serves for many women as the beginning of a period of transition, a kind of death and rebirth from one way of being in the world to another. The dark tunnel of unknowing serves as a threshold into a new world that can only be reached by the pain of giving up previous presumptions. The period of mourning the old way and the lost world is real and difficult.

The major shift during this period is that our ego, our I self, is no longer the center of our selfhood. We acquire a new center, a new way of being in the world in which we can get some "role-distance" from everything that happens. The old games and the old scripts lose the power they may have over us. We become free from the trap of egotism and are able to see it as a vital, necessary part of our development, which we have grown beyond. With this new shift, at long last we have the potential to be free floating, to fly and soar as the birds. The cage of the ego is the most seductive of all cages, and working free of it can be as complicated as developing it to start with. Our goal is to reach inside toward our creative depths.

Ann Schoonmaker

THE CHANGING OF THE TASTES

June Keen

With the advent of my 58th year, which coincided with our fortieth wedding anniversary, I began to develop a taste for the bitter. Bitter—I wanted the flavor of intensity; a sharp taste biting my tongue. After all I had bitten my tongue most of my unexpressed life. My taste buds craved endive, capers, and the bleached out inner core of iceberg lettuce. I sought foods, which puckered up my mouth and left me with a wistful look. Bitter herbs. I ate burned toast and drank dandelion tea made from the leaves I picked in the yard. I went around chewing on leaves of sage. Nothing more bitter than sage. The years with Henry had become bitter and my taste buds told the truth when my conscious mind could not face what we had become.

Perhaps the most obvious telltale sign was my closing down the kitchen. Across the course of my life, I had made enough fried chicken dinners and roast beef, mashed enough potatoes and baked enough apple pies to fill up any man. Now I was finished. The kitchen brimming with familiar, comfy smells from the perpetual cook, the symbol of happy hearth and home was no more. No announcement, no strike, no fanfare, I just stopped.

I began reading cookbooks from foreign lands with exotic ingredients that I had no notion of, nor any intention of trying. I existed on nasturtium sandwiches, endive soup with dill and anise and cream cheese, lox and bagels with jasmine tea. I sampled all the exotic fruits I could garner—ordering from catalogs, strange and unusual foreign ingredients simply because I loved the romance of their names. I planted herbs in manure and dark soil and experimented with broths and vinegars with strange and heady flavors.

Needless to say, these changes in culinary behavior did not bring about marital delight. But Henry didn't comment. Which was not surprising. We had stopped talking to each other years ago except to defend any previously undeclared small turf. Living a roommate relationship for years, each with our own individual life, which rarely encompassed the other, I took away the last common arena—dining together. I suppose he accepted my withdrawal from him in the kitchen as he had finally accepted my withdrawal from him in the bedroom after he had several affairs.

Other tastes began to change also. Clothes are such a visible sign of identity. I went from being this frumpy woman wearing beige and brown polyester to the woman who wore "gypsy." I tore up my Montgomery Wards charge card and became a worldwide shopper haunting the resale shops at the local college. I went for long flowing skirts, with tops of natural materials—the more brightly colored the better. Many of my new finds bore tags saying "Made in India" and other exotic countries.

I tuned into my body's wants and found that were many sensuous bones in me that sought expression. Tactile tastes like velvet, silk, rayon, replaced the ever-practical polyester. For this first time in my life, my closet was so awash with colors and textures that it looked like an abstract painting. Birkenstocks now became my shoe of choice. I had enough of cramming my bunioned toes into pointy-toed high heels. The wide, ugly shaped shoes made it much easier for me to roam through the woods. With my newfound colors, I fit right in with the brightness of the fall leaves. The crimson and yellow sumac trees were no match for my brilliance of colors that Gauguin and Van Gogh would die for.

My daughters were appalled with my changes of taste. "Muth-urr", they would say using their well-practiced phrase of their teen years. "Muth-urr, are you going to wear that? Moth-urr, why don't you do something with your hair? Do you have to wear those jangly bracelets? Muth-urr, Becky saw you walking barefoot in the park again. Muth-urr, what is going on? You look like an old hippie! Muth-urr, are you out of your mind? What will the neighbors think?"

The daughters, worried about my becoming dotty in my old age, consulted their psychiatrists and their teen-age daughters. They had endless arguments with me about my not getting the proper nutrition and the color and style of my hair, which was going back to its natural state of frizzy and gray. "Why wasn't I at church last Sunday? Did I know what Mrs. Hawkins had said about me? And the bridge club was gossiping about me. How could they hold their head up in town? What had happened to their middle class, conservative, Betty Crocker mother? MUTHURR!"

I couldn't tell them, because I didn't know. It was so gradual a change, from the inner me to the outer transformation and such a necessary one, that I didn't even know what was happening. Or that anything was happening. All I knew was that in this time of my life, my tastes had changed. My style had changed. I was no longer frugal, frumpy and fixated on living through others. I had become someone I had waited all my life to become.

Now I craved the bitter, the loose, the unconventional, the freedom of the body unencumbered, the spirit wild and free. I wasn't the same woman that I had been at 50 or those years previously. Thank goodness, I did not remember much about her, but I don't think I liked her that much. Nor many of those earlier definitions of myself.

Maybe the changing of the tastes was brought about when my best friend died that year after a long painful bout of cancer. Maybe it was because I had conformed enough for one woman living 58 years on this earth taking care of others. Maybe it was because I could not stomach another Tupperware party even though the merchandise now being giggled over by middle-aged Midwestern women was intimate apparel instead of plastic bowls. Or that I was so bored with the same-o, same-o that I was ripe for change. Whatever it was, I had had enough. And I wasn't doing it any more. I resigned from church committees and the bridge club. I canceled my subscription to the *Better Homes and Gardens* and signed up for *Utne Reader* and *Crone Chronicle*.

It wasn't even a rebellion, you know. What I was doing did not seem to be born of anger. It was more like a subtle, silent revolution where I stopped doing for others and started doing for myself. A revolution of self when I put down the apron and the committee lists and picked up brightly colored scarves and long, dangling earrings and started moving my body to the beat of the music.

My son and I had lengthy conversations about Doris Lessing, different ways of meditation, the best place to buy organic produce and Eastern gurus who had sex with their devotees. My son had studied martial arts and had just completed an oriental massage course. My tired body became the guinea pig for him to practice his newly learned massage techniques. With my son—my first-born and my co-conspirator in all things new, came my learning of the gift of receiving. Just receiving the good things that came my way—the colors, the scents, the sensuous delights. For the first time in my life of 58 years, I delighted in being able to receive gifts without the compulsive, guilt driven need to give back.

I cleaned closets and attic with a religious fervor, calling my daughters to warn them that sentiments of a lifetime were being tossed and to come claim what they could not live without. I haunted antique stores and brought home exotic remnants of other people's lives to fill the nooks and crannies that had turned up with the rigorous housecleaning. I found joy in old jars colored blue, green or amber. I tossed out the beveled edge glass coffee table and brought home an ancient wooden traveling chest to rest my fire engine red painted toes on when I was weary from my adventures of finding out who I was.

Finally Henry, who had not noticed anything about me for years, could not ignore my seemingly eccentric behavior. I had set up a small altar in the corner of the spare bedroom complete with a scarf with long black fringe, incense, daily fresh flowers and a bronze statue of Quan Yin and a picture of the Blue Medicine Buddha. I spent some portion of my morning there meditating on the vastness of the universe and the simple joys of my childhood.

That Blue Buddha I put on my shrine did it to Henry. "My God, Edna, you're not getting religion are you? At your age? Why the Hell, is this blue guy's picture in here? What's this crap about you checking out all the metaphysical books at the library? And I'm hungry! There is nothing in the refrigerator except some green things in bags. What is going on?"

I could only shrug my shoulders, not knowing how to talk to this man who came from another planet. This man whose bed and life I had shared for nigh onto forty years and who hadn't the slightest clue who I was. At times, I would catch him watching me with a puzzled look on his face.

It was the girls, of course, those traditional daughters who decided that Henry and I must publicly celebrate our fortieth wedding anniversary with a party. "Don't want one," I told them. "It's a lie, hypocrisy, to pretend that we are happily married. We've lived separate lives for years. Don't know why we've stayed together. Never had a reason to go our separate ways I guess. No party, do you hear?"

But no. They wouldn't hear about it. Caught in their illusions about celebrating the success of their parents who had stayed together for forty years, the girls began planning the party over my protests.

"Well, you can have it without me. I won't come. I'll run off." I threatened, giggling at the prospect of the wifeless anniversary celebration. But, I did give in to this convention of the celebration of my marriage of forty years. Something about not wanting to embarrass the father of my children. Owing him at least that much for giving me these three marvelous beings who had graced the various stages of my life. I recognized that my daughters, stuffy as they were, had turned out just like my former self, living the small town life as I had done at their age. And for all their nagging and worry over me, I saw them as splendid human beings. Still part of me grudgingly said that if I had to go, at least I wouldn't allow myself to have a good time. I couldn't be a hypocrite and pretend to be something that I wasn't.

So with family and friends about, we did the traditional opening of the gifts and laughed at the jokes of the difficulties of men and women living together in relationships. When someone yelled out for us to share what was the secret of a happy marriage and how had we managed to stay together all of those years, I froze. I just shut down unable to speak any positive messages about the institution called marriage and the hand that life had dealt me.

Henry put his arm around me and smiled. "Well, it was touch and go at first whether she would have me or not. She could have had any beau she wanted but somehow it was my good fortune she chose me. We've had a good life together. Our kids—couldn't have finer kids. Their success is her doing. Her values. She kept the family going. She's put up with me now through thick and thin, through good years and rough ones. The year I lost my job. That heart attack scare a few years ago. Just look at her! Look at how she shines. I don't know how I had the good luck to get such a woman. Don't always agree with her. Can't figure her out most of the time. Don't even talk to her much. But she is a fine figure of a woman and I'm proud to have lasted this long with her." He turned to me and said, "I wish us many more years."

Then I did something I hadn't done in years. Something I'd forgotten I knew how to do. I blushed. My face became as red as the silk fuchsia dress I was wearing. The tears came quickly to my eyes. My son broke in to save the moment saying, "Hey, how about some of that cake!" and everybody laughed and cheered. Turned out to be not such a bad party after all. Friends ,and family gathering around. Laughter. Connection. Communion.

So now Henry and I are moving into a different stage of our lives. All his energies stay at home. He seems to have given up the foolishness of his early years. He still watches me as if he is trying to figure me out. We talk more than we have in years. Occasionally we share a moment of two of intimacy. I've even considered talking to him about going to that new marriage counselor Betty and her husband liked.

I still crave the taste of bitter as I now celebrate the changing of the tastes and the bittersweet of being who I am. My wardrobe, as well as my daily existence, continues to become livelier. My daughter spies tell me that the local bridge club no longer finds my behavior or attire newsworthy.

Now and then, I reflect on the dull brown hen of a woman I used to be. When I count my daily gratitudes, I am thankful for that day when I first started to crave the taste of bitter. All those sage leaves that I chewed seem to have rubbed off on me. Sage, well named, in these years of becoming and accepting how I will play out my older years. For bitter herbs, when chewed enough, become sweet.

A DETERMINED STRENGTH,
A DIFFERENT LIFE

Joyce Kovelman

Alice is a special lady whose wisdom lies on the other side of words. Alice is 57 years old and lives in California. She is my identical twin. Nearly twenty years ago, Alice sustained a serious head injury while teaching a physical education class to high school students. Following this accident, her life was never the same. She tried many times to return to teaching, but found that she could not. Her doctors were unable to effect a cure and so, Alice sadly took a disability retirement, divorced her husband, and remained at home.

Five years ago, as I prepared for a holiday get together in my home; Alice arrived at the door with lip dangling and leg dragging. I stared at her in horror. I immediately called her doctor and arranged to bring Alice to the hospital the next morning. The next day, after extensive testing, doctors determined that Alice had a brain tumor in the left frontal lobe. They scanned all over her, and fortunately no other cancer was discovered. A biopsy revealed the nature of the cancer and radiation therapy was the treatment of choice. Alice was given a prognosis of one week to three months; she returned home to die. The radiation effected a cure that was to last four and one- half years. Alice smiled. She always knew she would live.

Then last November, Alice informed me she was almost "cured" since four and one-half years had already past since the tumor was first discovered. She was on the home stretch and close to the five-year mark. Our family began to breathe a bit easier.

A week later, on Thanksgiving Day, Alice arrived at my home. I was surprised to see her in a wheelchair, but was aware she had experienced some recent difficulty in walking. She seemed quite lethargic, but the busyness of the holiday and the arrival of my other guests kept me from concern. Following dinner, one of my sons and my friend, Father Peter offered to help me take Alice home. We managed to get her into my small, compact car, but encountered enormous difficulty in taking her out of it. Suddenly, all three of us realized that Alice was frightened and near panic. We all began to suspect Alice was paralyzed from the waist- down. It took five of us to finally transfer Alice from my car into her home. After the initial shock, I contacted her neurologist and arranged to transfer her to a hospital the next morning.

The next day, we learned Alice had a second tumor, this time on the right side of the brain. A biopsy revealed that it was the same type of tumor that she had previously, and that very little in the way of treatment was available. She could not have any more radiation, and we learned that chemotherapy was not likely to be successful for her type of cancer. Together, Alice and our family determined there was nothing else, medically, to do for her. Again, Alice was sent home to die.

Alice was very depressed. Depression also echoed and reverberated through our entire family. Alice was reluctantly transferred to a skilled nursing facility when her condition deteriorated and she became more depressed. Several months passed and her prognosis indicated 3-6 months of life. No more. Alice did not want to die. I suggested that she visualize a pink "Pacman" devouring the cancer cells and cleaning up the debris. "Couldn't hurt, and there are absolutely no bad side effects," I offered. This seemed to be the only type of treatment available. It made all of us feel there was still room for hope! With great sadness, I contacted Hospice and arranged for their assistance.

As soon as the Hospice workers came on the scene, Alice's demeanor changed. No longer depressed or lethargic, she suddenly began to fight back. She was determined to live and to return home. She wouldn't hear of any other idea and steadfastly and resolutely held to her goals. Everyone noticed an immediate change in behavior. A few months passed, and Alice seemed not only emotionally better, but also physically better. She was more interactive and her cognitive processes were returning, intact. Everyone sensed something was happening. We contacted her doctors and arranged for another MRI to ascertain her status.

Following the MRI, I was informed that this second tumor had disappeared. I couldn't believe it and was afraid to share the news with Alice, fearful that it was somehow a mistake. To quell my fears, the doctors agreed to do a second MRI a few weeks later. And, once again, there was no evidence of any brain tumor on the MRI. Alice had a "SRC" (spontaneous remitted cancer). A miracle had truly transpired.

I was delighted to share the news with my twin sister. Alice didn't seem too surprised. She had suspected that she was healing. Still, she shyly shared that she did not know how she got well. I suggested that an unconscious part of Personhood knows how to heal and cure us, while the Conscious Self does not. Alice was incredibly positive and determined to be healed, although she did not know if it were possible. We decided to thank the part of her that had allowed her to heal. She had received a blessing.

Alice is continuing to surprise everyone. Paralyzed from the waist-down since Thanksgiving, it seemed most unlikely that she would ever walk again. But Alice is determined to see what is possible. With the help of the nursing staff and her physical therapist, Alice can now move her legs. She is not quite able to walk alone, but she can transfer herself from bed to wheelchair and back. It is enough to allow her to return home. Alice smiles. She knew she would not die and that she would, one day, return home. She just knew.

There is thorough and ample documentation of Alice's second tumor and follow-up MRI's that trace its progress and final disappearance. Doctors are totally amazed and unable to say what enabled a miracle to occur. When you see Alice, though, she shyly smiles. She has not remained static despite her physical difficulties. Her flexibility of mind and spirit has helped her combat severe challenges to her body. She has gone past help-lessness into taking charge of her life. No giving up here. She knows what she wants. Alice is going home!

WISE WOMEN ON MOVING THROUGH FEAR

When I dare to be powerful—to use my strength in the service of my vision, then it becomes less and less important whether I am afraid.

Audre Lorde

Nothing in life is to be feared. It is only to be understood.

Marie Curie

Do what you feel in your heart to be right—for you'll be criticized anyway. You'll be damned if you do and damned if you don't.

Eleanor Roosevelt

The only way to go through fear is to go through it. Holding my breath and my nose and jumping right in, if that's what it takes but going right in and doing it. After I spend some time caught and paralyzed in my fear thoughts, something in me shifts. Then I grit my teeth, squint my eyes and say, "Enough! I'm going through this!"

Gerri McKelsy

Fear. What is fear? It is only physiological arousal with a message attached that I'm not safe. Well I can decide with my conscious mind whether I'm safe or not. I breathe to get that adrenaline rush under control; I look at the fear message with a jaded eye. I evaluate, decide if there is actual danger or only perceived danger. Then I act. Fear is just some dumb irrational belief in me that is begging to be faced.

Judy Reynolds

You are not a psychological victim, but a situational victim. Do the mourning for the situation. The situation is not the problem; the coping is the problem. Pain is a piece of something—the coping with the event and the loss that occurred during the event. Pain worked through becomes part of your curriculum vita. Put it away as part of your past years.

Virginia Satir

Inner healing is a ladder, not a single rung, a process, rarely a one-time event.

Ruth Carter Stapleton

All shall be well, and all shall be well, and all manner of things shall be well.

Julian of Norwich

"Now It Is My Turn," Said the Little Red Hen

Jane Evans

The muses of Elderhood came and spoke to me:

"Old woman, you have been too long good.
You don't have to be good anymore.
Your too much goodness is reflected in your dowager's hump,
Your age-worn hands, your breast cancer,
Your loneliness, as you sit alone in the dark,
Your martyrdom, which stinks of rankness and bitterness,
These are but remnants of the you who sought your identity in
    others.

Your larders of yourself are empty.
You have put in a lifetime of goodness.
For the sake of your parents,
For the sake of your man,
For the sake of your children,
You, a woman always being there, waiting, serving, doing for
    others.
Tears, hidden away or falling down the familiar creases of the face.
Your opinions denied by sense of duty and fear or criticism.

Woman, who are you if you are not good?

Define yourself now in your own terms.
Others have defined you,
Your culture, your society said who you must be.
In your goodness, compromising your own definition of self.

The time is long past for meanings from others.
No more interpretations given by an age gone by.
This now time is for you.
Who are you, if not for those others?
Who are you not, if for yourself?
You have been too long good.
Old woman, you don't have to be good anymore."

5 Ls to Live By

As grandmother-crone, she majors in fun, play and laughter. "Outrageous" and "disgraceful" is this wise older woman (wow!) every day words in her vocabulary. These words also describe many of her actions. They can't fire her.

At 50, she threw a birthday party for herself and a dozen friends at a lovely Honolulu hotel radio breakfast show. The dining room included a panoramic 180-degree view of Waikiki Beach. She wore a purple muumuu and a red straw hat with the price tag still on it. Her birthday gifts were generally wrapped in black. Her kids gave her a framed copy of Jenny Joseph's poem," When I am an Old Woman I Shall Wear Purple." Her sister gave her an unneeded cane, denture cream and other products associated with aging.

That celebration perhaps initiated her unofficial rite of passage from motherhood to crone status. Later that year, she attended the birth of her first biological grandchild. "Awesome to the max," is how she describes that incredibly special moment in her life. Today, she has nine wonderful league-of-nations, multi-ethnic grandchildren in two blended families.

In the next half decade, she faced five life-changing happenings including a heart attack, a broken ankle, breast cancer which involved a modified radical mastectomy, retirement, and the death of a daughter. The first two events slowed her down; the cancer shook her to the core and forced a re-sorting of priorities. Retirement precipitated radical transformation.

The cancer and premature retirement prompted a dream, which she worked to fulfill, a one-woman photo exhibit, *Making Memories,* which offered an opportunity to say *Aloha* to her beloved islands. A retirement party followed. The theme of "When I am an Old Woman...Purple" promoted delightful silliness and fun.

She and her soul mate pulled up stakes and moved from Hawaii to the mainland to embark on an entirely new adventure. Within a year, they had visited 26 states in their RV before settling in Arizona. As a "tropical hothouse flower," she needed warmth and blue skies.

Her life was filled with Caribbean and Mexican cruises, a hot air balloon ride, visits with her three children and grandchildren. Then...the death of her 31-year old daughter devastated her. No woman should have to bury a child. It isn't in the natural order of things. The adult child, an insulin-dependent diabetic since the age of 12, succumbed to the complications of her disease. Her heart gave out while she was waiting for a kidney transplant. She had just been accepted to law school.

Her mom's heart flinched again under the stress and she ended up in the hospital with a heart incident, unable to attend her child's memorial service. She drew great strength and new purpose from a grief support group. She truly realized one only walks this way once, that the years here on earth are not a dress rehearsal.

About this time, she also learned of the Crone movement sweeping the country, that truly honors the wise elder woman and respects her wisdom. Reading, learning helped her to find new direction on her life's journey. She jumped into active living again with both feet. She teaches Aging to Sageing at a local community college. She has written and published travel and crone-related articles, is helping to establish a crone speaker's bureau, and with a friend, has developed a Certified Crone (C.C.) certificate. The new initials replace those earned in college that are old and no longer needed in retirement. She also conducts dream collage and fun, play, and laughter workshops. She served as activity coordinator for the RV park where she lives and has just completed an intergenerational romp novel.

She had another dream of doing a standup comedy routine on stage. She recently fulfilled that dream in a fun way through a talent show in the RV Park. Some may feel it was a nightmare rather than a dream come true. She takes time to blow bubbles, dance (hula, line, and ballroom), fly kites, and to make magic in her life. She talks with school age girls about being the best they can be. She shares information about Hawaii, the aloha spirit, and island culture whenever there is an opportunity. She facilitates a writer's group and a crone group in her community.

In her Ageing to Sageing classes, she developed a 5 Ls of Living program. She lives what she teaches. She has 1) learned to 2) loosen up, to 3) live, to 4) love, and is working on 5) leaving a legacy, sharing her wisdom and joy of life with others. She be me, gael Mustapha, C.C., 57.

JOURNEY TO THE ISLANDS OF THE GALAPAGOS

Lynne Namka

Return, return to the deep sources, nothing less
Will teach the stiff hands a new way to serve,
To carve into our lives the forms of tenderness
And still that ancient necessary pain preserve.

May Sarton

In the night sky, a dark, raging buffalo visits,
Humping my hurting body,
Snorting, pawing the ground,
Invoking my sleeping volcanic core.
Rendering me bruised, sleepless, questioning,
Some of me calls him pain;
His true names are defense, resistance, fear.
This volcanic island sways in rhythm
Reeling with the dark forces of the universe.
Grotesque aspects of my defended self,
Are frozen in swirling blackness.
Molten emotion erupts leaking
Through the tear-shaped craters of the soul
Inviting the demonic forces within me
Which must be danced.
Knowing the chaos, the richness,

The suchness of the origins of Life.
Of this I came, for this I came,
To emerge single celled, out of the ferment;
Bleak, barren, stark, raw sexual energy, yet ever
Pregnant, with a small sign saying
"Under Development."
The now-graying buffalo kneels to pray,
Camouflaged against the primordial darkness
Humbled, surrendering to that ancient necessary pain.
The white buffalo emerges.
Light, filtering and dancing through archaic waters,
Portraying the ever-changing patterns of my life,
Sinking effortlessly on the nonshores of time and space,
I enter the great sound.

WITHERING FACE, FLOWERING SPIRIT

Skye Blaine

One afternoon, in my early forties, as I stood in front of the mirror, I noticed with horror that the skin around my mouth was breaking down into fine wrinkles. The light is stronger and less forgiving at that time of day, and I was wearing my new reading glasses. My denial fell away in that instant. My whole body reacted; my heart rhythm jumped, solar plexus tightened, and stomach felt slightly ill. I was not escaping aging...I was becoming my mother's face, my grandmother's face. I wasn't ready.

The frown line between my brows came first, and at a young age, by twenty-two I think. My dad had the same frown line, and I had consciously modeled mine after his. As a child I looked very young for my age; I was also the youngest in my family and the neighborhood, and was certain this was a disadvantage. I felt that lines would help me look older and add character, and I cultivated them, using my face in an expressive way that encouraged their development. The frown line added a serious, thoughtful quality. The smile lines, like sunrays around my eyes, became indelible in my thirties. I didn't mind them because I had memories of elder women in my family, especially my Aunt Betty, and her smile lines were the signature of her warmth and joy. Yes, wrinkles have been gathering on my face, faster this decade than before.

In my experience, when something is taken away, there is often a gift in return. It is not always obvious, and it may not be easy to receive. Sometimes I must stalk it as a hunter stalks prey, quietly, with patience and above all, endurance. Clearly my young adulthood was over. Gone, I knew in that moment, and not recoverable. Living in this culture, where aging is not honored, this new experience of myself came with both fear and pain. What did this mean in my life? The stalk began.

First there were periods of intense sharing with my women friends. It was too fresh, too fierce a feeling to share with male friends yet. That would come later. My women's lodge gathered sixty women together for a Council on Aging. We invited active old women in their seventies, eighties and nineties to share their wisdom with us. We risked plumbing the depth of pain we collectively have that in this culture, female beauty is synonymous with youth. With quiet rage, women shared feelings of becoming anonymous, unseen. We spoke how we want to be when we are very old. We laughed and cried together; we danced our beauty. I discovered there were many of us on this path exploring, seeking a new way. It helped.

Around forty-six, the deepening began. I needed large chunks of time alone, and my husband, what a wonderful partner, encouraged my claiming that time. I had a strong need to sleep alone, and felt as though I was birthing myself anew. My spiritual practice reawakened with a richer vitality. My listening changed subtly and powerfully as an unquenchable thirst for truth emerged.

I developed peace with my wrinkles as I turned forty-eight. The movement of my life stemmed from a different, deeper source. I began to feel called to places, people and work, by my inner listening rather than personal desire. I felt a creative quickening inside that was reminiscent of the surges of energy I had as a teenager. My uncertainty, shyness and self-consciousness left. I started writing; I knew as a small child that this would develop, as I grew older. I began telling my truth firmly, clearly, and lovingly—a crone voice.

Approaching fifty-one, I feel like ripe, mature fruit that is ready to nourish others; it is clearly time to give back. My community is asking for that giveaway just as I am ready to respond. I am an energetic light for others and can bring objectivity well seasoned with love. I can accept the mantle of mentoring another. These attributes are abundantly available in my friends as well.

We are seeking to move into our elder years in ways that speak of far memory and distant times; there is resiliency, deep power, and courage. We are choosing to allow the gray to emerge in our hair, and face lifts are not a topic of discussion. So there, women's magazines! This culture will have empowered, elder, wise women who claim their voice and the right to speak it, and we will not be invisible. Withering face, flowering spirit, how beautiful we are!

WISE WOMEN ON THE JOYS OF BEING AN OLDER WOMAN

Oh to be a woman at this time, this culture, this age. What excitement, what joys, what possibilities!

Anonymous

And only when we are no longer afraid, do we begin to live in every experience, painful or joyous; to live in gratitude for every moment, to live abundantly.

Dorothy Thompson

The only real security is not insurance or money or a joy, not a house and furniture paid for or a retirement fund, and never is it another person. It is the skill and humor and courage within, the ability to build your own fire and find your own peace.

Audrey Sutherland

What a wonderful life I've had! I only wish I'd realized it sooner.

Colette

I suppose—the moments one most enjoys are moments—alone—when one unexpectedly stretches something inside you that needs stretching.

Georgia O'Keefe

I enjoy being a woman of some fifty plus years. I have the best of both the male and female energies. I can be strong and tough and yet soft and feminine. I keep adding more to who I am; I'm filled up with experiences that show my competence in handling whatever is thrown at me. Woman! The word means empowerment to me.

Jane Evans

A salty is a healthy woman who is using the freedom of her independent, later years to belie the age/sex stereotype, She is celebrating her liberation from the dependence and caution of her childbearing years with what the late Margaret Mead once labeled "menopausal zest."

Catherine Bird

The chalice dwells within; the outer petals drip with sun-blown dew. Love remains the everlasting gift.

Flora Coblintz

Be happy. It's one way of being wise.

Colette

The Old Crone

There are positive aspects of being a frightening old woman. Though the old woman is both feared and reviled, she need not take the intolerance of others to heart, for women over fifty already form one of the largest groups in the population structure of the Western world. As long as they like themselves, they will not be an oppressed minority. In order to like themselves, they must reject trivialization by others of who and what they are. A grown woman should not have to masquerade as a girl in order to remain in the land of the living...

There have always been women who ignored the eternal youth bandwagon and agreed to grow up, who negotiated the climacteric with a degree of independence and dignity and changed their lives to give their new adulthood space to flower and function.

Germaine Greer

YES TO CRONESHIP!

Lynne Namka (author credit)

"I'm an Old Crone now. I can be anything I want to be. I can say anything I want to!"
Overheard at a women's gathering

Woman's evolution comes by moving through the major developmental life stages from dependence upon others to independence of self and interdependence with others. Each stage contains within it conflictual patterns that produce crisis, which affords the leaven for a higher state of growth. Many women understand the wisdom of giving up muscle power for mystic power. They complement the exciting journey of claiming their age while maintaining a youthful outlook. Through processing of the challenges of a lifetime, women acquire wisdom and a deeper aspect of the personality comes forth—the Old Crone.

Who is the Old Crone? The word crone comes from *crona*, which means crown in the Germanic languages, signifying royalty and wisdom. The Old Crone is the archetypical image of becoming spontaneous and free from the detrimental programming of society. She is a richer aspect of our younger self—a wiser, freer and more connected version of who we used to be. She has life's experiences and maturity on her side. She has learned much in her years of living and always looks to continue to grow and ripen. She exercises the gray matter between her ears learning something new each day knowing that mental activity promotes sound health. She reduces hassles in her life. She has learned to make more efficient responses to stress. She continues to learn, adapt, push and keep her balance as she walks on the shifting ledge of the challenge of her later years.

The Old Crone is the saucy complement to the compliant "good little girl" self. She refuses to give in to the unrealistic needs of others and become a dry shell. She is opinionated, alive, free, and juicy! Others are attracted to her vibrancy. In her expanded state, the youthful Old Crone sends forth magnetic energy that draws others to her. She makes others feel visible just by focusing her attention on them.

The prerequisite for harmony and peace is to journey through the dark side of one's personality. For the Old Hag is hiding in the shadows. To become the Wise Old Woman, we must walk through the dark path of the Old Hag. The Old Hag is one aspect of what Carl Jung called the "Shadow side" of the personality. The Shadow represents the primordial qualities within us that are part of us but do not fit with our "ideal self." Everything we personally hate about ourselves fits into the Shadow Self. Ann Kreilkamp's definition of crone is "She who eats her Shadow."

The Shadow parts are those disowned selves that we deny and push down because they are painful to face. The forces of our destruction lie hidden in this unknown part of our nature, which are so often denied and resisted. As the saying goes, "What we resist persists." These disowned Shadow parts of ourselves hang around until we call them forth and examine them.

During the second half of life we can risk letting the darkness come in, so that we can learn to view it in a different way. As Ranier Maria Rilke said, "Our deepest fears are like dragons guarding our deepest treasure." Addressing the Shadow is the only way to find the true richness of who we are. Finding strength through adversity, confronting the dark, and restoring the whole is the challenge of the mature woman. We must go through the Shadow if we are to move into full maturity.

Without this most difficult task of going into our personal dungeons to address our monsters, we cannot become whole and integrated. When the baser parts of our nature are explored, they become transmuted. The fear of the dark is no longer held at bay. Exploring the Shadow is to pass through death into rebirth and transformation. Elizabeth Howes and Shelia Moon say it well in their book *The Choicemakers*, "But these dark powers have their particular healing qualities, if you learn of them and sacrifice your narrow ego defenses. You are the child of below as well as that of the above. Remember that."

The Old Crone has come to terms with her Old Hag self. One of the many paradoxes of being a woman is the interplay of our Old Hag self with the wisdom we innately know. When we get into our Old Crone wisdom, the darker side of our nature no longer horrifies us. The Old Crone has learned to value the uncomfortable aspects of her nature as simply being human. She becomes free from the fears both self generated and those imposed by others. By looking at the Old Hag within each of us—the darkness composed of fear, anxieties, angers and depressions, we older women can find power. We must go into our time of darkness to find the richness that we are. Based on the rich inner life, we can finally let go of the tyranny of being caught up in what other people want or in our own selfishness.

The Old Hag, if ignored and denied, turns into bitterness, anger and despair in later life. As we bring forth the Old Hag in ourselves and understand who she is, we grow and stretch. That which we disliked most in our mothers can come forth in us as the Old Hag. We are mystified to find that we are her in a different form. We reluctantly and grudgingly play through her issues.

We all have some piece of the Mother Wound. Control, judgment and victim thinking come forth as troublesome symptoms to be worked out. For underneath the Old Hag lies the Wounded Child limping and defended with armor who cries out to be healed. The child must be heard and addressed if we are to feel good about ourselves.

Older women's stories are rich in Crone imagery and metaphors that assist us in healing our Wounded Child. Stories of Cronehood beckon us to remind us of the depth of our wisdom within. So Sisters, let us hear, let us hear. Let the story spirits speak out telling us of those Crone stories of old that connect us all. Come closer, come closer...

Look At Me—This Is Who I Am: The Charge of the Crone

Antiga

I am the beauty of the dark moon and the dark earth beneath
    your feet.
I am rest in the evening of your life.
I am the skin and bones of your existence.
I am She who is weathered by time, aged to perfection.
I am the midwife to the dying, promise of life everlasting.
All acts of birthing and dying are my rituals.
I am Hecate, Erishkegal, Baba Yaga, Menat.
I am Sedna, Sjheilg-na-gig, Sibyl, Edda, Weisse Frauen.
I am the darkness you fear and welcome.
I am the freedom to express your essence.
I am the courage to cast aside the opinions of others,
as you live life according to your own plan,
in tune with your own truth.
I am the wisdom that can guide the world.
I am the energy of the old,
the knowledge of when to cut the cord.
I was with you at your birthing and will be with you
to ease the transition of your dying
into the world beyond.

TRANSFORMATION

Rucy Neiman

Do not think for one moment
that this Crone magically appears
She comes from the digging in the soil,
the eating of the seed,
the intense and enormous learning
gleaned here in the pain of darkness
which is not darkness
but another plane, another way of seeing
where we eat up our suffering intentionally
in love and learning.
And each learning is an opening
to Power,
each page turned a step to wisdom.
This Crone who come
has had to be developed with difficulty,
to be nurtured with pain,
to be sought out and prompted.
Do not think for one moment that
she is a gift.
She is hard earned
and she is worthy
because I have taken this clay
and formed her.

THE CALL OF THE CRONE

Ann Kreilkamp

The Crone came to me in a dream in July 18,1989. I don't remember the dream. I do remember being roughly shaken awake from behind by a huge black bird. The situation felt urgent. She cawed at me, *Wake Up! Wake Up! It's Time! It's Time!*

Though shocked at her roughness, I was not surprised by the message. The Crone energy is so powerful, so magical, and has been so long buried in the collective unconsciousness, that once aroused, I knew she would wake up the world—or bury it in her fury.

For decades now, I have been fascinated by the archetype of the Crone—loving Her, fearing Her. All my life I have wanted to be old. Even as a child I knew: only then would I be released from the nonsense that goes along with being female in this society. Only then, would I be fully myself, inside and out...

We are shifting from an exclusively biological understanding of being female to one, which speaks to the mind and heart and soul. We reflect upon the cycles of our lives and seek a larger awareness. This search enlivens us, quickens us. We shake off others' opinions and speak our own truths. We laugh to remember how we cried. We honor the mystery. We surrender to love, and open ourselves to co-creating a new Earth, a new humanity.

Excerpted from Founder's Statement: Crone Chronicles: A Journal of Conscious Aging.

BABA YAGA

Antiga

Listen wild women and you shall hear
    the tale of a crone-
      old, wrinkled with age
      whose visage is fearsome, some say
The tale of a goddess as wild as you
Baba Yaga is her name.

    Baba Yaga Baba Yaga

    Bag 'o bones Bag 'o bones
    Haggard old hag
    Fearsome grandma
    of the deep Russian woods
    They scare young children
    with an awful fate
"Babe Yaga will eat you if you don't behave."
    Baba Yaga Baba Yaga
    Bag 'o bones Bag 'o bones
    The way to your house
    Is strewn with sticks and stones
    But when one arrives
    A surprise is in store
    A house on chicken legs-quite alive
    Twirling and spinning around and around

That responds to the sound of a voice
Saying these magic words:
"Little hut, little hut,
Turn your back to the forest
Turn your face toward me, your guest
I ask for help on my quest."

The yaga is skinny, the yaga is old. The yaga is bold and her magics are many. Most likely she'll agree to a request if the seeker will do as she asks, performing the tasks however easy, arduous, or improbable they may seem; however short or long the work lasts.

Now she rides high in the sky in her large iron cauldron. She sweeps away all traces of her travel with her broom as she flies. Her long hair flies in the wind as she goes.

Where does she go?
What does she see?
She flies to the mountain
She flies to the shore
She flies to the north
She flies to the south
She flies to the mouth
of the river joining the sea
She flies to the east
She flies to the west
She spins around three times to bind her spell
She watches to see who passes the test
She finds those who honor her not
who make fun of old women
bowed down with age
who beat their wives and children.

In her cauldron Baba Yaga carries skulls full of live coals that leap to do her bidding. When she casts her eye on those who hate women, she burns them to a crisp in a flash. Baba Yaga cackles as they return to earth in an altered form. Baba Yaga has no mercy for those who mock the young ones, the old ones, the foreigners, the women whose life is hard. Yes, she's a dangerous old hag all right. Nothing escapes her keen eyes.

> Baba Yaga flies through the air
> the wind in her hair and
> Whirlwinds follow in her wake.

Baba Yaga protects courageous women who work hard without pay or appreciation, and then she rides home to her house deep in the woods surrounded by a fence of skulls that glow from within with live coals. Her house on chicken legs runs to meet her. It is delighted to greet her as she returns. Her supper simmers in a cooking cauldron as she lies down to rest.

They say her house on chicken legs is a terrible spot. She will kill you if you come too near. So beware to those who care naught for the Goddess and those She protects. But if you speak the right words, her magic is yours.

> Baba Yaga Baba Yaga
> Bag 'o bones Bag 'o bones
> An apron, a kerchief, a wrinkled face
> air filled eerie tones.
> She sleeps by day
> Rides high in the sky by night
> Can you see her silhouette against the stars
> that hang in the sky?

Flying in her cauldron one evening, Baba Yaga overheard a gruff voice below: "Woman, why do you let the baby cry? What kind of a mother are you? Can't you shut the brat up?"

Marushka, the mother's voice pleads. "The baby is hungry. I've had no food in a week. My milk is running dry."

The man knew this was true. He hadn't eaten either but his hunger turned to rage. He grabbed the baby and began shaking her, harder and harder and harder. The mother screamed, did her best to grab the baby from his grasp. He was big and strong. She could not get the baby back. She knew he'd kill the baby if this went on. Wild with desperation, she called for Baba Yaga. "Grandmother, save my child."

In a flash of lightening, Baba Yaga was there. She gave the father quite a scare. He dropped the child. The mother caught her and fled. But Baba Yaga was not through with him. She bid the live coals leap from the skulls and burn him to a cinder. She cackled and cackled as his ashes fell to the earth. She swept them out the door and left them to fertilize the garden.

The mother heard the cackle but did not turn back. The life of her precious child was at stake. She ran and ran. She had no idea where she was going. She ran and ran and then she ran some more. As it began to get dark, she found herself in the fearsome forest, where wild animals lived. She ran until she dropped from exhaustion. She fell onto some soft pine needles where she and the child fell asleep.

They awoke the next morning rested, but hungry. She began to look around. She saw some wild berries, which she knew they could eat. She thanked the Earth Mother for Her bounty as they ate. With strength to walk again, she picked up her baby and realized that a miracle had happened. Her milk was flowing once more now that the fear for her child was gone. Or was she in an enchanted forest? "Thank the Goddess again," she cried. Rested and refreshed, the woman picked up her child and set out again. She didn't know where she was, so she let her intuition guide her.

When she came to a place where the path forked, she picked the most interesting path, the most mysterious—whatever caught her eye—way to go. After a time, she came to a clearing. What she saw surprised her mightily. There was a fence topped with skulls. And stranger yet, there was a house running around on chicken legs. She could hardly believe her eyes. By now it seemed certain that she was in an enchanted forest. She stared and stared at the house, which was running around the yard. Inside was an old hag with a cauldron. Yes, she had seen this hag before. It was none other than Baba Yaga, the fearsome crone that she had heard many tales about. But, contrary to the awful tales, Baba Yaga had saved her child. As Baba Yaga landed her cauldron, she became bold and asked: "What am I to do now?"

Baba Yaga replied gruffly, "Why should I answer you?"

"Because I need help and because I ask for it."

Baba Yaga's tone of voice softened and she said, "You can stay with me. I need help around the house. Your child will be safe here."

Marushka was pleased and started right away making the house on chicken legs more inviting. She gathered flowers in the woods and placed bouquets around the house. She washed and ironed the curtains. She put the feather bed out to air. The greatest magic of all was food. All she had to do to cook a pot of buckwheat groats was to put one grain into the pot. As it cooked, it became enough for them all to eat. She worked and played with her child and did not realize for a long time that she missed her husband not at all.

Many evenings were spent by the fire as Marushka and Baba Yaga exchanged stories of their lives. As they grew closer, Baba Yaga began to teach Marushka magic. As Marushka became more and more adept at magic, her daughter grew into an older child and then into a budding teenager. Magic was an everyday part of her life. When her first blood began to flow, they all planned a ritual to honor her entrance into womanhood.

It happened in the spring, just as the flowers in the woods were beginning to bloom. The young woman invited women whom she had come to know while learning magic, for her mother and Baba Yaga were not her only teachers. The young woman prepared herself for the ritual by a bath to wash away what she would not need in her grown up life. She put on a red robe to acknowledge the beginning of her adult life. All of those invited to the ritual gathered in a secluded place in the woods, a place where much magic had taken place. The young woman walked around the circle and greeted each guest individually. After they had cast the circle and called to earth, air, fire and water, they called the moon goddess to be present for it was she whose cycle the young woman was entering.

During the ceremony, the young woman took the name she would use for some years to come. She named herself Divozenky after the Bohemian wild women of the woods who knew herbal lore and sought to understand the secrets of nature. Divo is what they soon began to call her.

They made a birth canal with their legs and as Divo struggled to get through, they squeezed her between their legs as she passed through to show her that birthing is a difficult process. One of the women was at the end of the birthing passage to welcome her into womanhood with hugs and kisses and a song sung at first bloods rituals. After birthing her, they put her in the center of the circle and danced around, singing another song improvised around her new name. The merriment and dancing went on for a long time.

When they had danced and sung until they were tired, they celebrated by giving Divo gifts. Some brought her material to make robes. Some brought her jewelry that they had made especially for her. Some brought her images of the Goddess to put on her altar. Others brought flowers and food. They all brought their wishes for her adult life.

"May you always love yourself first."

"May the Goddess protect you wherever you go."

"May you find friends and lovers who respect you and help you create your life as you want it to be."

"May you live comfortably in your body and continue to love it."

"May your body be strong and healthy."

"May you cry freely when you need to."

"May your anger empower you."

"May your magic benefit those who are lonely, poor or disheartened."

"May your spirit soar to the stars."

As an acceptance of her new status as a grown woman, Divo gave each of the guests a gift that she had made. They opened the circle to end the ritual and Divo walked back to the house on chicken legs with her mother and Baba Yaga.

Years passed and Divo became as accomplished an herbalist as Baba Yaga's first daughters had been. She was more and more gone as she lived her own life. The wishes of the witches at her first blood's ritual were coming true. Baba Yaga and Marushka were both glad and sad to see Divo grow up and be on her own. Marushka and Baba Yaga were more and more alone in the woods as Baba Yaga grew older and older and older. It became clear to Baba Yaga that it would soon be time for her to move on to her next existence. One night she said to Marushka, "Will you become the next Baba Yaga?"

Marushka was shocked. She somehow had believed that Baba Yaga would stay with her forever. She did not want her to leave. Baba Yaga said, "My time is nearly here. Prepare a farewell gathering for me. Invite my cronies to a party. I want magic to be with me as I make the passage."

Grieving as she did so, Marushka did as Baba Yaga had requested and gathered together those with whom Baba Yaga had practiced magic for so many years. Baba Yaga lay in her bed as they arrived. She greeted each one and asked that they all gather round her bed and lay their hands on her as they cast the circle. There were exactly thirteen women present counting the Yaga. The women caressed her ancient body and Marushka climbed into bed with Baba Yaga. Sitting at her head, she cradled her body and rocked her as the others continued their soothing touching. They sang songs of passage and spoke words honoring her life.

Baba Yaga bid farewell to each woman and thanked her for her caring and companionship. She accepted and acknowledged the farewell that each woman bid her. Baba Yaga slowly sank into what looked like a deep sleep. Yet her eyes were open. As they watched, they saw her spirit leave her body and fly out the window into the night sky. They watched as she flew toward the stars and her body remained behind. They cried to see her leave. They would miss her deeply.

Marushka and the other women prepared her body for burial. They dug a hole in the earth. Wrapped the body in one of her favorite quilts and lowered the body into the earth that she had loved where she had lived so long. Marushka felt herself to be a different person.

Now it was she who was Baba Yaga.

WISE WOMEN ON KNOWING THE DARK SIDE

Shyness is your way of getting your feet wet toe by toe and testing the water. You learned to survive in childhood by looking around and watching instead of doing. You learned not to take a big leap and risk. When one toe goes in and it feels good, the foot follows, then the rest goes in. It is a way of saving on towels. If you don't like it, you don't have a full retreat. Testing of the waters is a way that is safe for you."

Virginia Satir

I have a right to my anger, and I don't want anyone telling me I shouldn't be, that it's not nice to be, and that something is wrong with me because I get angry.

Maxine Waters

Your anger is a manifestation of the body to give the message that it is out of harmony. Anger has an energy that needs to be transformed...As a human emergency system, honor your anger. Admit it and learn from it. Face angry feelings and communicate them directly to drain off the steam and the need to act destructively.

Virginia Satir

I know of no companion as terrible as fear.

Ida Tarbell

Ultimately we know deeply that the other side of every fear is a freedom.

Marilyn Ferguson

Nothing in life is to be feared. It is only to be understood.

Marie Curie

The open wound always heals. Stay with your pain; it has great gifts for you. You will always have enough energy for healing if you stay open. Stay open to staying open. Shift does happen.

Lynne Namka

There are three possible outcomes in each situation—winner, loser or learner. Feelings can be losing, winning or learning. I wish you learning from your feelings... To be conscious of the feelings and the body is to be mindful of the heart.

Virginia Satir

ARRIVAL OF THE CRONE

Persha Gertler

I feel Her
rumbling
in the fiery
underground
of rock and root
the dark abyss stirring
with all that is hidden.
In that deep place
I hear her—
a cackle I once feared
becomes music
a roar I once ran from
makes me tremble
with anticipation
a pounding of dancing feet shakes loose
the crust of the world.
I stand on the edge
and wait for the moonfire
of her wild hair
around Her lined, earthen face
Her radiant, mountain body
full of her stories and mine.
I wait, arms open wide,
and I say yes and yes and

step over the threshold
into the long night
that holds Her
the long night I have journeyed
all my life to find.

FULLNESS: THE CRONE AND HER SHADOW

Ann Kreilkamp

> Consider the Venus de Milo
> paragon of physical beauty.
> An immortalized marble ideal.
> Like a Platonic Form, this statue stands
> as a touchstone of western culture,
> guiding our perceptions to discover it
> in the ephemera of time, and then, often,
> attempt to hold it there,
> frozen.
> Now consider the flower,
> a physical ideal not limited to western culture.
> We zoom into the heart of a
> particular flower's inviolate sexual beauty,
> transfixed by exquisite color and detail.
> We want the beauty,
> and we want it to remain.
> How bittersweet!
> The bloom is so short,
> our communion,
> so fleeting.

Like a flower, a woman's physical beauty blooms briefly, and then fades.
Only the time-scale differs. What takes a few days for the flower may

extend into a few months, years, perhaps even a decade or two. Life molds and remolds our bodies to reflect what we have made of our hopes and dreams. Our faces trace the maps of our inner life.

The physical ideal, possible in youth, and which renders young bodies similar, also limits their expression. The bright innocence of youth's face transforms into a dance of light and shadow, as reflection teaches us subtle distinctions between them, and their integration. We learn to refine the dance, to move in directions unknown to us when we are young.

And then, there are those rare times, when Venus herself infuses us again, with a new love. A dear man or woman, a painting, a book, a child, a project—once again there is communion. We bloom into radiance. This time our skin glows with a light cultured from within. A beauty of spirit. Age has nothing to do with it. We are ripe now, full of ourselves.

GRANDMOTHER PROVERBS FOR THE SECOND HALF OF LIFE

The first fifty years of my life were for other people, these next fifty years are for me.

Gray is great. White is wonderful.

The older the violin, the sweeter the music.

Menopause is a time to be sexy, witty and wise.

The glory of aging is being able to speak your mind and be your most necessary self.

I am aging perfectly into my prime and on and on.

Things of quality have no fear of time.

Old age is a time to let the best of opposite gender behavior emerge.

One joy in this time of my life is to make others feel visible.

At last we have the time to find new and innovative ways to skin that proverbial cat.

Aging allows more time for a more elegant maintenance of the body.

As I learn my lessons in aging and wisdom, my peace increases geometrically.

Change is my middle name. At my age, it better be!

As we get older, we get better; we get more like ourselves.

Menopause is an achievement in a woman's life, which frees her to work, flirt and be wise.

Aging is losing the little self to go to the big Self.

Rich Valley After the Flood —name of a Chinese herbal soup for post-menopausal women.

These older years give me the time to see more of the Divine manifesting in me.

After fifty, its fun, fun, fun!

AFTER THE MENOPAUSE

Gwendolyn Purdy

after the menopause
I grew a soft big tummy
like a full-term pregnancy
my fertile wisdom bag
full of unborn poems
jiggling like jelly
cushioning my core
of sensuousness
I have become
a crone of abundance

Seasons of Crone

Dorothy L. Bray

Crone About Spring

I am on my morning walk. Spring is coming, maybe even here. The calendar says it is here, but calendars were invented too long ago to be relied upon today.

It is early in the morning, but the air is balmy with puffs of gray fog that are vying with the emerging sun for survival. The fog is losing. Soon the day will be clear and bright.

I am reliving other springs now: Springs from a long ago, Springs spent at my Grandmother Laura's house, Springs with the Aunts and Uncles and Cousin Helen. Springs when I was surrounded by a large extended family. And I remember rich details of the childhood triumphs and humiliations in the midst of this clan of first-generation Norwegians.

Springs when hobos would find the path to Grandmother's porch, from the old train depot a short distance away, never to be refused a meal, which they would eat out by the old cistern while Cousin Helen and I would peek at them from behind the shed in the back yard.

Springs when Easter chicks would be silently removed to the nearest farm. There were no tender emotional support conversations, adult to child, about the sudden losses of these feathered pets; there was not time for that in the no-nonsense Springs of the 1930's.

Springs which were as brief and treasured then as they are now.

The only difference between those long ago Springs and now is that past Springs were also part of the Spring of my life, and this Spring and those that I have left are the Spring of my Winter.

> More gracefully anticipated.
> More tenderly absorbed
>   and
> More poignantly felt.

Crone After Summer

> I saw them this morning.
> Myriad of black dots in the sky.
> Flocking, Flying.
> How can summer be gone?
>
> But
>
> There is a chill in the night air
> When the sun is down–A warning.
>
> And
>
> Here and there, a bright red-gold
> flashing in the dense green– a harbinger.
>
> And
>
> Last night when I was in my bed,
> I heard acorns on my roof
> Heavier than rain;

Sharper than hail;
Clack, clack, clack:
Falling, Rolling, Returning

And

. In my neighbor's yard, a tender young
Apple tree has lost a whole limb
To ripened birthing.
All around me I see.
Summer, summer,
Come back, come back.
How can you leave me?

Crone Towards Winter

The crispness of the air is echoed in my joints: A frosty edge that glints discomfort, but melts off during the day–offering a false sense of well being for short time –'til dusk.

Nature is far kinder to the bouffant coifs of the trees, giving them red, oranges and yellows in the fall of their lives, but leaving me homely streaks and wisps and shades of grey which sift through my dark hair like the ashes in my fireplace.

I watch the chipmunk that lives under my side deck carry acorns back and forth. Back and forth she goes, harvesting the abundance that fell so short a time ago.

Regrets crowd my memories and, arm in arm, memory and regret, like the chipmunk, march back and forth in my mind, back and forth. Did I harvest the abundance of life? Or did I trample through the fields of my youth, crushing promise underfoot: next time, next year, next harvest.

But now, now the harvests to come are not an endless line of time, but measured out, to be treasured: picked, carried home, tasted, shared, savored...

Winter will be here soon, knocking at my door with a hoary fist: peering through my windows with white, soft, blind eyes, seeking me out, pointing icicle fingers at me.

I am feeling alternately safe and then, suddenly, alone and frightened.

I want to stay in my home, my shelter, my place, but instead I venture out, and brush aside the icy hand, to go past and beyond the blind, white eyes and march into the winter of my life.

Aged Bones—Supple Minds

There's something about affirming the totality of yourself, the way you are authentically. I am myself at this age. There's something about that that's enormously liberating. You realize you don't have to live up to some of the things that have haunted you, that have driven you.

And then you become a truth-teller in a way. And you can risk yourself in new ways.

Betty Friedan

THE GIFT OF CONTRACTION

Lynne Namka (author credit)

"You are as young as your faith,
As old as your doubt,
As young as your self-confidence,
As old as your fear.
So long as your heart gives forth messages of love, hope and cheer,
So long, then, are you young."

Anonymous

Growing old gives the opportunity to make aged bones, which then can come a loosening of sorts. Late Winter Woman uses her time for removing the unnecessary clutter and collections of a lifetime. Removing the weight of past debris is freeing, just as cleaning our closets allows for simplicity and order. The older woman has gained true wisdom when she truly appreciates the simple things of life. Having seen and done much in her life, she knows true value. She is content with having little and savoring much. As singer Roberta Flack said, "Simplicity is strengthening." Late Winter Woman has cleaned the closets of her life from emotional baggage. And with the cleaning out comes a knowing of oneself and the youthfulness of spirit. Joy follows.

Older age can be a time of creating a vacuum so that richness can come in. We open up to the vacuum and send something out to invite new things in. We give up parts of ourselves to gain wisdom. We release that which is unnecessary to make room for another level of awareness.

Grandmother Joyce Kovelman tells us, "All birth is proceeded by contraction. Expect resistances. They reveal where and how we need to grow."

Losses, which inevitably come with aging, can be watched with a Zen-like detachment as we step back and look at the aging process. Taking stock of the role of loss in life, we can sit back and say, "Oh, that's what it's like to have loss of vision. Ahhh, now I have lower energy. So this is what it is about. So, I'm getting forgetful. Well, some things I don't need to remember. I need to make better choices as to what is memorable."

The wise older woman decides to change her outlook on any losses of her body and concentrate on what she can do. She drinks deeply from the cup half full, seeing the fullness of it. During those difficult times when the cup appears half empty, she does what she has to do. Emptiness then becomes her lessons.

Late Winter Woman actively creates a new vocabulary, a new language to signify the transitions in her life that are born of loss and of adventure. In maturity, she finds a philosophy about losses that allows her to find daily happiness no matter what her body state. She finds meaning in life even during the dying process.

Like Grace, dying of a painful but swift death, in a nursing home. The harder she suffered, the more angelic she became. She knew what she was doing in her dying. She had work to do just as she had worked her life long. Now her work was dying. She did not make others breathe her pain. She followed her instincts of living a good death as she had achieved living a good life. Those around her were rewarded by witnessing her achievement. She touched their lives deeply. Quietly, with dignity, she was transforming her being into that which was purer, refined. She was completing her process while earth bound, preparing for that which came next for her. She simply followed her spirit home. A death well achieved.

The opportunity to make aged bones is a rare privilege in itself when you consider the alternative. A woman's life, if done with grace and spirit, can become an alchemical process of purifying and rarefying matter into spirit. Conscious aging dictates that you cultivate your mind. Be aware of its unconscious renderings of both the destructive and health evolving aspects. The independent turn of mind makes both the conscious and unconscious decision to become its own alchemist to find the Philosopher's Stone.

The following stories are written by or about women who have lived seventy years plus on the earth allowing their wisdom process to take full effect. Older women's stories reflect the wisdom sought and found in their lifetime. So take a deep breath, Sisters. Clear your mind and lean forward. Hear another story. For one story begets another. Listen well to what these wise women of later life have to say. Let us hear what our elders have to tell us.

Wise Women on Sorrow

For every ailment under the sun,
   There is a remedy, or there is none.
   If there is one, try to find it.
   If there be none, never mind it.

Mother Goose

Sorrow has its reward. It never leaves us where it found us.

Mary Baker Eddy

We learn as much from sorrow as from joy, as much from illness as from health, from handicap as from advantage—and indeed we learn much more.

Pearl Buck

Life is either a daring adventure or nothing.

Helen Keller

The main thing in one's own private world is to try to laugh as much as you cry.

Maya Angelou

Life is what we make it. Always has been, always will be.

Grandma Moses

There is no limit to human suffering. When one thinks: "Now I have touched the bottom of the sea—now I can go no deeper," one goes deeper. And so it is forever…Suffering is boundless, it is eternity… What must one do? There is no question of what is called "passing beyond it." This is false.

One must submit. Do not resist. Take it. Be overwhelmed. Accept it fully. Make it part of life…Everything in life that we really accept undergoes a change. So suffering must become Love. This is the mystery. This is what I must do. I must pass from personal love to greater love. I must give to the whole of life what I gave to one. The present agony will pass—if it doesn't kill. It won't last… Life is a mystery. The fearful pain will fade. I must turn to work. I must put my agony into something, change it. "Sorrow shall be changed into joy." It is to lose oneself more utterly, to love more deeply, to feel oneself part of life—not separate.

Katherine Mansfield

ON YOUTH

Anonymous

Youth is not entirely a time of life—it is a state of mind.
It is not wholly a matter of ripe cheeks, red lips or supple knees.
It is a temper of will,
a quality of the imagination,
a vigor of the emotions.
Nobody grows old by merely living a number of years.
People grow old only by deserting their ideals.
You are as young as your faith, as old as your doubt,
as young as your self-confidence,
as old as your fears; as young as your hope, as old as your despair.
In the central place of every heart, there is a recording chamber;
as long as it receives messages of beauty, hope,
cheer and courage, you are young.
When the wires are all down
and your heart is covered with the snows of pessimism
and the ice of cynicism,
then and then only have you grown old.

EVER-CHANGING WOMAN

Lynne Namka

Sitting in my rounded house of earth,
Well warmed by ancient rituals of bath and oatmeal,
I am struck by the memories of my life.
Remembrances of painful incidents are sweetened this morning
By the reflection of the many versions of myself,
Of the different names I have called myself across the course of
   my life,
Who I have become just for the going through it all.
Somehow, having gotten through the years of the locust,
Somehow, getting through those lean years of spirit,
Into these elder years of satisfaction which share my table this day.
I am Ever Changing Woman,
Learning to be true to Self even in the face of perplexity.
I allow this lot that has made up my life,
Both the sublime and traumatic, that the fates have cast for me.
Sitting and listening to the joyful song of a desert mockingbird,
Now, as I prepare for the Great Transition,
I let go of the woman stories of my life.
In the quietness of this round mud house
Surrounding me like the womb I once knew,
Late winter sun filtering in this late winter span of my existence,
I celebrate this knowing that allows the warming of my bones.
I have returned to the kiva of my soul.

WISE WOMEN ON AGING

Most men prefer... a real woman. And real womanhood doesn't even begin to come into full flower until 40.

Jackie Collins

Staying young is an inside matter. Your body grows old but your body is not you... You do not grow old. You become old by not being young.

Wilfred Peters

It's time that we start searching for the Fountain of Age, time that we stop denying our growing older and look at the actuality of our experience and that of other women and men who have gone beyond denial to a new place in their 60s, 70s, and 80s. It is time to look at age on its own terms, and put names on its values and strengths, breaking through the definition of age solely as deterioration or decline from youth. The problem is how to break through the cocoon of our illusory youth and risk a new stage in life, where there are no prescribed roles, no models, nor rigid rules or visible rewards—how to step out into the true existential unknown of these years of life now open to us and find our own term for living them.

Betty Friedan

We post reproductive women are far from helpless. For we bring a lifetime of ingenuity in managing at all income levels and all levels of health or disability. We're very hard to frighten, and a good number of us are as wary as the old female elephants who lead the pack. Some of us even find living alone as liberating as going to college the first time or cashing that initial paycheck.

Barbara Sagarin

The body is your instrument in dance, but your art is outside that creature, the body. I don't leap and jump any more. I look at young dancers and am envious, more aware of what glories the body contains. But sensitivity is not made dull by age.

Martha Graham

I refuse as I age to deny my years. When asked at 30, I'll be 30. When the question comes up at 45, I'll take 45. For what year could I subtract? The one in which my son or daughter was born? Or the year I first fell in love? How about the ones less favorable? Like the year I came down with pneumonia. Or one of those grief-filled years spent saying good-bye to someone close? Many I could choose the seemingly insignificant. That year I saw a falling star? Of the one spent not enthralled with life, just content with it? No, I think I'll keep them all, the good years, the bad and even the not so memorable. To deny one would be to deny myself. Because added up, they are my life.

Shelia Careara

CAUSE FOR PAUSE

Joan Weiss Hollenbeck

We have grown to an age when
our sisters die
and we find a part of us
goes with them.
How fitting to scatter ashes
at our beloved Moss Point
where growth groups gathered
these last twenty years,
when white shells hung around our necks.
We sang: "Listen, listen to my heart's song,
May we never forget you,
May we never forsake you."
A sister/leader has gone before us.
We stand in tribute
to breathe the sea,
to feel the salt wind;
to hear the sigh of the waves,
All this in our cause for pause.

AN UNLIKELY FRIENDSHIP

Lynne Namka

It was a wonder that Polly was sitting at Jo's kitchen table at all. "Other women were not to be trusted," mused Polly to herself. "I could never relax completely in the company of a woman." She had never had a close female friend. She had always chosen friendships with boys during her teen years and subsequently men. After marrying Brad, she came to the conclusion that a woman friend might be a threat to her marriage.

Women weren't safe to befriend. With her husband's roving eye, Polly found it prudent to exclude close friendships with women. Or maybe she had absorbed some of the pain of her mother who lost her best friend and her husband in the craziness of one felt swoop of a mid-life affair. With these attitudes of distrust, Polly had kept herself away from the close company of women.

Now there were different needs coming to the forefront. "Get yourself a support group," the therapist told Polly. "If you don't have support in your marriage, and you don't, look for it outside. Develop women friendships—good gutsy friendships." On some level, Polly knew he was right. A good, accepting friend of the same sex was the closest that you could come to fulfilling the universal childhood dream of having totally, loving accepting parents.

But the manifesting of this well-placed advice was another matter. Reaching out to other women was so risky for Polly. She had somehow passed her forty-plus years on earth without a close friend. On her part there had been tentative offers of friendship made and then withdrawn. Polly's outward manner of composure intimidated many women. Her retiring manner, a cover up for shyness and insecurity, suggested aloofness. Each unfruitful experience, each betrayal of her confidence by another woman had left her wary. Yet her loneliness drove her to continue to extend tenuous gestures toward other women of her age.

But it was not that way with Jo. Polly felt awkward yet somewhat comfortable in Jo's chaotic kitchen. Across one window was a shelf of plants growing towards the light. Hanging baskets dripped their dead leaves and lush greenery alike. There were several old stone jars, some corked, others with cattails and dried flowers sitting next to the small painted wicker rocker that was covered by a colorful afghan. In one corner were tasseled pillows and an old copper boiler spilling over with faded newspapers and magazines. A faded crocheted rag rug drew the room together in a warm, homey fashion. Despite the confusion and sensory overload, the room fit together.

Jo stood in the center of her creativity. She was rounded and unconcerned about the extra pounds that were gradually being added to her frame. She hummed as she poked around the various objects, clutter really, in disarray on the counter top. She padded through the room with the slip-slap sound of thongs gently spanking her heels as she put on the coffee and looked for cups without chips.

"I like this kitchen" thought Polly. Jo's house projected warmth and it felt real. "Perhaps I could learn about letting go of my compulsion to clean." She flashed back to an earlier memory hearing her mother proudly saying "How we keep house is a reflection of how we keep our lives." Polly thought of her own kitchen, organized and modern. Now that she considered it, it seemed rather cold and clinical. She wondered, "What pattern runs me that I need to keep everything so tightly controlled or I become unglued?"

Despite their widely divergent outlooks and personal styles, here they were sitting across Jo's brightly flowered tablecloth drinking coffee. Two unlikely friends. Opposites must attract. Polly appeared cool and pristine with an artificial veneer about her. Other women called her Polly Polyester behind her back. Perfect Polly Polyester. Given a different type of interests and support system, Polly could have been smug and self satisfied, telling other women who didn't have it so good, how good what they had was. But Polly had a streak of innocence about her despite her air of defensive sophistication.

Jo, on the other hand, was an earth mother: expansive, generous, flowing and disorganized just as Mother Nature. Jo was opinionated and active in causes that fit her lifestyle and politics. A former hippie, now studying for a degree in social work. She often took in waifs and strays to practice her theories, round out her days and avoid her housework.

They had met at the supermarket when a pyramid of tomatoes tumbled down as Polly chose one less blemished from the bottom of the pile. She looked up guiltily to find Jo's laughing eyes as the tomatoes rolled everywhere. They chuckled as they scooped them up, and Jo suggested that they make a fast get away.

"I just looked at you and knew," Jo said much later when they could talk openly. "Even with your perfect hair and clothes, somehow I knew that there was more to you. Something deep, born of pain, perhaps. But we sure look different on the outside! Maybe opposites really do attract."

The friendship was not instantaneous. First they had to cut through the layers of superficiality, strata of self-imposed artificialities of communication that women of the sixties used to define themselves. Friendship is a risk undertaken and survived for the fullness of both. It is a gradual opening up and a clearing out of the emotional debris that clutters the unexpressed heart just as spring cleaning pulls out the dirt and dust build up in a seldom opened window sill. Inviting a new friend into one's life has the possibility of allowing for crying and laughing at oneself.

But Polly and Jo were not at that level of understanding. Their conversation was still at the polite, superficial level. A nonsharing of sorts except for the facts. Questions such as "Did your son enjoy Boy Scout camp?" and "Do you have a good recipe for hamburger?" Polly was starting to feel more and more uncomfortable. Jo reached for the coffeepot and poured the steaming coffee into her mug brim full. As she moved from the counter to the table with the mug, her hand wobbled and the hot liquid spilled over, scalding her hand. The mug broke as it hit the tile counter.

"Oh, shit!" she yelled, and looked up to catch that look of dismay on Polly's face. "Well, it is now or never," Jo thought as she ran cold water over her hand and reached for the butter. "She's got to see me as I am. Take me or leave me. Jo grinned. "I always feel better after a nice, healthy cuss word. To get the pain and frustration out. For many years, I tried not to get upset when things went wrong." She moved to get the sponge. "But then something happened that made me see the futility of trying to be in control. It was one of the best things that ever happened to me."

As she mopped up the mess, she continued. "I had gone to visit my Aunty Dell who had just been admitted to the nursing home. She'd had a stroke and fell and broke her hip. Living alone, she had no one to take care of her. She was 86 years old and her mind was starting to slip a bit. Nothing serious. When I got there she was lying in bed fingering her patchwork quilt that was old and worn thin as herself. That old quilt was a little bit of home in that sterile hospital room. Its fragile, faded state seemed to echo Aunty Dell. And yet like her, it held character, real character."

Aunty Dell just lay there touching the quilt softly saying, "Shit, shit, shitty, shit." Over and over she said it. She pointed to her roommate and told me, "That old woman over there just keeps saying shit all day long. She don't know what she's saying." She pointed to the woman who was sleeping in the next bed. Aunty Dell laughed and clapped her hands and hit her knees. "Shit, shit, shitty, shit! The food here is shit. Look at all that shit over there. And the people are shit too." Her body rocked with laughter. "Shee-itt!"

Jo spoke, "Now I've known Aunty Dell all of my life and a straighter laced woman you have never met. I had never seen her cry or complain over anything. She never said a bad word about anybody, and Lord knows she had reason to with that husband of hers. Now they were coming out. All those stored up "shits." All of those bad things that had happened. All those years those 'shits' were kept inside just waiting for the right time and place. I watched her fingers stroke that quilt as if she were remembering each stitch and what it had meant to her. Each piece of patchwork, a compromise. Each stitch a letting go of who she was. She wasn't particularly angry, puzzled or confused as she just counted out those 'shits.'

'Shits' never expressed because a lady just didn't talk that way. 'Shits' over meals getting cold while waiting for her manfolk to come home. 'Shits' for giving away what pleasured you because you knew someone else wanted it. 'Shits' for clumsy, klutzy things you did like breaking your favorite vase. 'Shits' for all the remarks you let pass. 'Shits' for telling yourself that it didn't matter when it did. Now they were escaping. It took a stroke and old age and helplessness to allow them to come out, but here they were!"

Jo continued, "And it was okay by me! I thought that she had earned the right to speak those words squelched down. She deserved them and others deserved to witness them. She let the pain out. That squelched pain of a lifetime. I started to smile just thinking about it. Aunty Dell and I sat and laughed together. Others had laughed at her—the nurses and staff—at that senile old lady sitting and cussing. But I laughed with her and shared her delight at finally expressing her pain. I identified with her. I knew about that kind of life. The kind where you hold it all in." Jo continued. "I had always been that good little girl myself, never raising my voice, never saying no, always so pliable and agreeable. It was passed on to me by my mother, and here I did the same thing in raising my daughter."

"I looked over at Aunty Dell's roommate who had wakened and was sitting on the edge of the bed. She looked like a shriveled lemon. Her response to old age was to pull into herself and keep the world out. She had a dour look on her face as she sat there swinging her legs. Bitter. She looked bitter as if somehow life has slipped by without her savoring the flavor of it. I thought that I would much rather be like Aunt Del, even with her mind ajar, shocking people and laughing about it."

"So I joined her. I had some 'shits' inside of me that were unexpressed. Shit, shit, shitty, shit." We chanted together. Over and over. We must have said a lifetime of "shits." We laughed until the tears ran down our faces. The nurses came to see what the commotion was all about. They thought I was crazy too. That mental illness runs in the family! At the sight of each different nurse who came in looking horrified, we would go into hysterics again. A few caught the joke and joined in the merriment." Jo grinned.

"Aunty Dell died of a heart attack the following week. I was with her when she died. She hadn't had much humor in her life, losing her first baby when she was so young and putting up with her alcoholic husband and all. But we laughed that afternoon when those 'shits' came out. Laughed until we hurt. I like to think we made up for it—that serious, starched life she had chosen, that all women (good women, that is) of her day chose to lead in submission."

"At her funeral I wanted to stand up and shout, 'At least she got her 'shits' out before she died. She didn't die with her 'shits' left in her!' Of course, I didn't. Now I wish I had." Jo looked over to catch the question on Polly's face.

"Did all that cussing and laughing hurt her when she was so ill and cause her death? I don't know. I don't think so. But it sure helped me. Changed me. I went out of that hospital that day with a fresh outlook on cussing. And, more important, a fresh outlook on life. The relief valve of saying what you feel! Saying what you feel is like a pressure cooker that spouts off when it needs to rather than holding it in. 'Shoot' has never done it for me, nor 'heck' or 'darn,' Jo continued. "They just weren't strong enough to express what I really felt at that flash of anger. Now I let it go. I say what I feel, straight and loud. Whatever I feel at the moment. Don't feel guilty about it. Just let it go and bless Aunty Dell. And what I found is that I don't need to cuss much. It is the permission giving that freed me. That was her final gift to me."

Polly looked puzzled as she stared off into space. "Oh I could never... 'shit'?," she asked tentatively. "Shit?"

Jo nodded. 'shit.' she replied in an affirmative voice. "Life can be such 'shit.' And while we hold it all together by telling ourselves that it isn't. If we were just braver, stronger, prettier or whatever, we wouldn't have to eat all that 'shit'." That is the real 'shit' of life—putting ourselves down and eating 'shit.' When we finally learn to label the real 'shit,' then we can appreciate the beauty that is there for us too."

"Shit," agreed Polly. "Yes! Shit. Yes. Shit, shit, shitty, shit. Shit, shit, shitty, shit. Shee-itt!" They took up the refrain together. Again and again. Louder and louder until they were both holding their sides with laughter. "Oh, my side hurts." Polly pounded the table. Like first graders who have just learned a dirty word with a great need to shock themselves and others, they repeated it over and over. They tried to stop the laughter as if they were not allowed too much of a good thing. But every time they had it contained, they would look at each other and burst out again.

From that day on, there wasn't anything that they couldn't talk about. Polly had found her first friend. She and Jo found a common bond. Laughter and the recognition of being the same under the skin had fused the common bond of sisterhood.

WISE WOMEN ON SERVICE TO THE WORLD

When you help, you see life as weak; when you fix, you see life as broken. When you serve, you see life as whole. I think I would go so far as to say that fixing and helping may often be the work of the ego, and service the work of the soul. They may look different if you're watching from the outside, but the inner experience is different.

Rachel Naomi Remen

We cycle through patterns that bring us repeatedly back in the vicinity of whatever our nemesis is that we must meet and master...Life presents us with repeated opportunities to face what we fear, what we need to become conscious of, or what we need to master. Each time we cycle around the spiral path to the place that gives us difficulty, hopefully, we gain more consciousness and can respond more wisely the next time; until we can finally pass through that nemesis place at peace and in harmony...

Jean Shinola Bolen

Prayer worn hands and a rusty plow never got the crops in.

Brett Bravo's mother

We ought to come to our work as we come to a beautiful child, with reverence and love.

Mary Haskell

A woman does not have to do anything to become a healer or a shaman. Those terms are synonymous in most cultures besides ours. Modern Western medical situations understand that the healer is also shamanic. Shamanic, herbal setting, bone setting all go together. Every woman is a healer by virtue of having a womb. A woman transforms from maiden to mother to crone…There is something about going through menopause that changes a woman's energy in such a way that allows her to work very effectively as a healer. And not just for individuals, but for the community and for the planet as well.

Susan Weed

What do we live for, if it is not to make life less difficult for each other?

George Eliot

This is the difference in "total surrender." To accept whatever He gives and to give whatever He takes with a big smile. This is "the" surrender to God. To accept to be cut to pieces and yet every piece to belong only to Him is "the" surrender…to accept and to give whatever it takes… it takes your good name, it takes your health, it takes "YES." THAT'S THE SUR-RENDER, and that is the clue. Then and only then are you FREE.

Mother Theresa

We can do no great things—only small things with great love.

Mother Theresa

As A Grandmother, I Write My Story

Anonymous

AS A GRANDMOTHER
I WRITE MY STORY

NOT AS A WRITER
NOR AS A STORYTELLER
BUT WITH DEEP CONVICTION
I WRITE FOR MYSELF
TO HEAL THAT PLACE IN ME
THAT HAS BEEN COVERED UP
HIDDEN, THAT WAS VIOLATED
AND RUN FROM
SO LONG AGO

FROM THIS SPACE
I TELL MY STORY
OPENING THE DOORS TO LOCKED ROOMS
THAT SEEMED IMPOSSIBLE TO BE ABLE
TO WALK THROUGH
BEFORE NOW

I CAN NOW REMEMBER AND ACKNOWLEDGE
MY PAST, LOOK AT IT, SENSE
HOW SECRECY FELT

HOW FEAR REORGANIZED IN MY MIND,
IN MY BODY
HOW HOLDING ON FELT
HOW IT FELT TO BE IN TERROR

IT TOOK ME A VERY LONG TIME
TO ALLOW MYSELF TO REMEMBER THIS
THESE SEVENTY PLUS YEARS
THESE YEARS HAVE GIVEN ME THE WISDOM NOT TO HIDE

BECOMING AN ELDER MEANS
NOTHING CENSORED
INTEGRATING MY EXPERIENCE
MEANS BEING AN ELDER
THIS BEING AN ELDER
GIVES ME THE TOOLS TO WORK WITH MY TRUTH
NOT TO FILTER-BUFFER OUT WHAT LIFE
HAS GIVEN ME FOR LESSONS

IF THERE IS A MESSAGE TO OTHERS
FROM MY STORY- IT IS,
IT IS NEVER TOO LATE

TO WORK THROUGH THE SUFFERING OF THE PAST
IN FACT—IT IS NECESSARY
TO WORK THROUGH
AND UNDERSTAND IT
IN ORDER TO LET IT GO
AND BECOME FREE AND CLEAR
NOW IN THE PRESENT
IT IS MY BIRTHRIGHT TO DO THIS

MY JOURNEY HAS INCLUDED
THE INVESTIGATION OF MANY CULTURES
AND MEANINGFUL SYSTEMS
AND BELIEFS
PERHAPS I WAS MOTIVATED BY
MY EARLY SORROWFUL EXPERIENCE
TO TRY TO UNDERSTAND
WHAT IS POSSIBLE.
THE BEST WAYS TO BE
TO BRING MEANING AND VALUE
TO MY LIFE

RINPOCHE WROTE:
THERE IS A PURPOSE TO OLD AGE
A FUTURE TO BE FULFILLED:
THE FIRST PART OF LIFE IS FOR LEARNING
THE SECOND PART OF LIFE FOR SERVICE
AND THE LAST TIME IS FOR ONESELF

I HAD NOT LEARNED MUCH ABOUT
HONORING ONESELF IN THE LAST STAGE
OF LIFE FROM OUR YOUTH-ORIENTED CULTURE
AGING WAS LINKED TO DECAY
DECLINE, DEPRESSION AND DISCOURAGEMENT
IT WAS NOT LINKED TO SELF EXAMINATION
SELF-REMEMBERING
HONORING AND LOVING THE SELF
WE WERE TOLD
"KEEP IT QUIET"
IT'S TOO LATE TO INVESTIGATE"

I LOOKED BACK
REMEMBERING THE SECRETS
THE MYTHS, AND PAINFUL ISSUES,
THE CATACOMBED MEMORIES
THAT I NEED TO PROCESS AND
TO LET GO
IN ORDER TO LIVE WITHOUT FEAR
(DR. ELIZABETH KUBLER-ROSS SAID SPEAKING OUT OF ALL
    UNRESOLVED
ISSUES IS MANDATORY IN ORDER

TO LIVE UNTIL YOU DIE
AND TO DIE WELL)

MY STORY HAS BEEN ONE OF
SEARCHING FOR
MY TRUTH, MY POTENTIAL
WHILE REMEMBERING MYSELF
EVEN THOUGH IT GUIDED ME
THROUGH DOORS HEADING TO DARKNESS
IT ALSO GUIDED ME
THROUGH DOORS OF LIGHT
HOPING FOR UNDERSTANDING
MORE CLARITY AND REPOSE

AS A GRANDMOTHER, MOTHER, WIFE
FRIEND, AUNT, ARTIST, LOVER
WORKER, COOK AND LOVER OF BEAUTY
I WISH THAT LIFE WILL CONTINUE TO HAVE
THE MYSTERY AND POTENTIAL FOR ME
UNTIL THE LAST, DEEP, SOFT BREATH

MAY WE ALL BE FREE FROM SUFFERING
. MAY WE KNOW PEACE.

SAVING WHAT'S GOOD

Angela Pechenpaugh

Morning, after a bad dream,
then reading the paper
with its usual stories
of local tragedies,
violent loss of life of the young,
national politicians true to their greed,
heedless of most people's needs,
or one where someone
has done an act I cannot comprehend
so dark at its roots,
the torturing of a horse to death,
I come upon Helen
on my way up the road.
She's stooped over the neighbor's yard
plucking pears from the ground
and putting them in a bag.
Years I've seen them fall
and rot on the parking lot.
I ask her if she saves the bruised.
"Oh yes," she says, "I cut off
the bad part. I put them up."
She goes on with her task
saying, "They fall so fast."
Helen, in her eighties, with

a farm in her past
is salvaging what can be used
and concentrating on that.
She's preserving sweets for winter
which will be harder.
She's giving me hope.

A CRABBIT OLD WOMAN WROTE THIS...

What do you see, nurses, what do you see?
Are you thinking when you are looking at me—
A Crabbit old woman, not very wise...
Uncertain of habit, with far away eyes,
Who dribbles her food and makes no reply
When you say in a loud voice—"I do wish you'd try."
Who seems not to notice the things that you do,
And forever is losing a stocking or shoe.
Who unresisting or not, lets you do as you will,
With bathing and feeding, the long day to fill.
Is that what you are thinking, is that what you see?
Then open your eyes, nurse, you're not looking at me.
I'll tell you who I am as I sit here so still;
As I use at your bidding, as I eat at your will,
I'm a small child of ten with a father and mother,
Brothers and sisters, who love one another.
A young girl of sixteen with wings on her feet,
Dreaming that soon now a lover she'll meet;
A bride soon at twenty—my heart gives a leap,
Remembering the vows that I promised to keep;
At twenty-five now, I have young of my own,

Who need me to build a secure, happy home;
A woman of thirty, my young now grow fast,
Bound to each other with ties that should last;
At forty, my young sons have grown and are gone.
But my man's beside me to see I don't mourn;
At fifty once more babies play round my knee.
Again we know children, my loved one and me.
Dark days are upon me, my husband is dead,
I look at the future, I shudder with dread.
For my young are all rearing young of their own,
And I think of the years and the love that I've known.
I'm an old woman now and nature is cruel—
'Tis her jest to make old age look like a fool.
The body, it crumbles, grace and vigor depart.
There is now a stone where I once had a heart;
But inside this old carcass, a young girl still dwells,
And now and again my battered heart swells.
I remember the joys, I remember the pain,
And I'm loving and living life over again.
I think of the years, all too few— gone too fast,
And accept the stark fact that nothing can last.
So open your eyes, nurses, open and see
Not a crabbit old woman, look closer—see ME!

WISE WOMEN ON RELEASING THE NEGATIVE

No one can make you feel inferior without your consent.

Eleanor Roosevelt

If you've ever contemplated revenge, beware of where your thoughts might lead... If you are very angry and your walk is a long one, you will need nourishment on your expedition, in which case you should pack a picnic lunch...If your regrets linger, if you cannot find inspiration in solitude, then you still have much to learn from the writers and the poets and the cooks on becoming the artist of your own life. The things that never can come back are several, and you can never recreate the past. But you can shape your own future. And you can make a cake... Eat the cake slowly and consider how you might perfect the art of living.

Jacqueline Deval

Nothing has more lives than an unforgiven sin or error we refuse to correct.

Mary Ann Ward

The psychological problem of forgiveness is seeking for and facing that which must be expiated, that which is knotted and crossed and crooked in both the interior and exterior life. The religious problem of forgiveness is the bringing of the crooked things into the presence of God, so that they may be accepted, reconciled and transformed. Jesus defined forgiveness as the taking of action in a new direction.

Elizabeth Howe & Shelia Moon

Our greatest task is to have the courage to face the thing that rises within us, whether it takes the form of doubt, which must be thought out, or the knowledge of unacceptable things within ourselves with which we must reckon. In this way only can be found the acceptance of greater consciousness.

Frances G. Wickes

NANA

Cathyann Fisher

In her advancing age, she let it all go,
talked about the advantages of a
fat butt, how dresses hang better without
all of that extra material hanging down low,
signifying what isn't there.
Crone as sage.
I have missed those types of
advice-that-I will-ignore-it anyway
until-I-have-lived-it conversations.
Real-woman talk.
We have to start younger
in these conversations,
find old women in homes,
strangers, if the others have gone.
Find women who have been
at each stage, fully alive
from life force, who know
and remember,
maiden to mother to crone,
who can say it should be this way
without shame—
like it is better to have a fat butt,
because she does not have to impress anymore.

OLD BONES SECRETS:
GOOD GENES, CAPACITY TO BE HAPPY

gael P. Mustapha

She doesn't feel almost 90 years of age. She has all her own teeth, tonsils, and appendix. She's never had surgery. She's tiny and petite and looks years younger than her driver's license says. Her arthritis allows her to bowl but not to scrub pots.

Lilah Holt, born May 31, 1906 in Anaconda, Montana, still has an uncanny ability to be happy, to get excited about life. She claims her mind isn't as quick as it used to be, but she plays cards, the piano, and talks to herself to keep the gray matter stimulated.

"I collect people," this charming, active woman who summers in Montana and winters in Arizona said. She never had children but has a little girl named after her. She is an aunt to siblings' children, but is also "aunt" to extended family "adoptees" picked up along life's road. She was the oldest of five children. Two brothers have passed away. A younger sister and brother are still living. Her father lived to be 90. He was a big influence in Lilah's life. She finds it hard to believe but exciting that she will see her dad again after death. She looks forward to that occasion.

She still lives by his advice to "try every day to make someone smile." "I recently told a gal I didn't know at a luncheon how lovely she looked. The woman seemed astounded. Maybe no one ever told her that before. I'm so glad I did it." Her own smile is infectious as she talks of her "guardian angel" ranger lady friend in Montana who checks on her regularly. Her guardian angel's parents have "adopted" Lilah. "It's fun having parents again," she twinkles.

Despite what she would have you believe, her memory is keen. She recalls making a birthday cake for a nephew on his first birthday. That nephew had a son who had a son who now has a son. Lilah and her late husband Joe, for many years, took that nephew on camping and fishing trips. Lilah laughed, "That young boy had perfect table manners. I took him to fine restaurants. He was a perfect little gentleman."

She also remembers an elementary school classmate. "We must have been in first grade...just learning to read. Johnny was a much better reader than I was.' She grinned, "Would you believe we used to sit in the two-holer outhouse on my dad's property and watch the world go by?" She left the area at the age of nine. She missed her friend, Johnny. When she was 14, she returned to the town and was very excited about renewing her friendship with Johnny. She was filled with teenage anticipation about the outcome of this meeting. She had curled her hair just so and wore a pretty new dress with flowers on it. "Imagine my chagrin when I saw him and he was still in short pants. I'd grown up. He hadn't." Her eyes twinkled. "I didn't give him much thought after that."

Lilah's first job was playing piano for the silent movies "when Mary Pickford was popular." She and her late husband Joe were married 63 years. He was an electrician with Montana Power. "He had a good job. I had my beauty shop." She ran her own business for 40 years; has now been retired from the shop for 25 years. Lilah and a dozen other Montana women worked hard to ensure passage of laws related to standards and licensing for beauticians. She studied with some of the best stylists in Hollywood and New York. She modeled hairstyles too. "I had lots of thick red hair." It is still unbelievably thick, dark and luxurious.

She believes her mother led a dull life. Lilah determined to "live" a fuller life. As a child, she overheard her mother say, "I had five little mistakes." In her child's mind, she sensed getting pregnant wasn't a good thing, was maybe the worst thing you could do. She and Joe both came from large families. Rhythm was about the only form of birth control available. "We just never had children."

She was quick to add, "We had love. Once you have it, it's with you forever." In her mother's day, those words, "'I love you' were never spoken but you knew your parents loved you. Thank goodness for the freedom today to express our love openly." She stressed the importance of sharing those words and meaning them with friends and family.

"Another thing, most people, especially seniors, don't like to talk about," she said, "is death and dying." She added, "Joe and I were like that but he made arrangements so I'd be taken care of. " We were fortunate. With his job and my business, money was never a real big problem for us. We weren't rich; money wasn't a big worry."

She shared her loss about Joe's passing. "No open casket, he was cremated. I want to remember Joe as he lived." In her career, she often worked with the undertaker to make up those who passed away. It didn't bother her then, but she followed her own personal choice of cremation for her own loved one. Pausing, she noted, "Sometimes, it's hard to be a widow in our couple-oriented society. Old couple friends may drop you when your spouse is gone. That can be lonely, hard."

Self-confidence is important to Lilah. Her participation in activities and organizations helped. Lilah is proud of the fact that one of her bowling teams placed fourth in the season. There were 24 teams in that league. She bowls with the Elks and Ladies League on Fridays, with her church league on Tuesdays, and subs for another senior team on Mondays. She's been called the "Queen of the Bowling Center." She won the Senior Olympics in her age division several times a decade ago. "Now they don't have a bracket for my age," she quipped.

Moving from the past to the present, Lilah credits her long life to good genes. She also firmly believes, "Jesus loves me, this I know, for the Bible tells me so." She sang in the Green Valley (AZ) Community Church Choir for 15 years. She was active in community affairs including the Toastmistress organization.

She talked about life's little lessons; things she has learned and believes should be passed on. "When you are hurt or upset, do nothing until time goes by. Ask yourself what part you played in this situation? Then, work at resolving and forgiving."

So how does her age truly affect her? "Well, I fall asleep sometimes while eating or while just sitting in a chair. It is strange to wake up on the floor in your own home. Fortunately, I have thick carpet." She has taken a couple of tumbles in public places recently. Fortunately, she's ended up with only scrapes and bruises rather than broken bones. It can be worrisome, she admits. "I've slowed down but I can still get out and about, enjoy people, and live fully."

As to leaving a legacy and facing the time ahead, she changes her will from time to time as appropriate and works with her finance man. She hopes to leave something for her church and her family. More important to her is encouraging people to keep a diary or journal, a written record for those coming up. She said, "I wish with all my heart that I had done that. It is so important and it helps you keep track of events, feeling, and thoughts."

Lilah concluded, "At this age and stage, I have no major goals. I've traveled, had a good life. I have a great capacity to be happy and I'm not afraid to share or to face what the future holds."

Risk Taking at 101

Jean-Noel Bassior

At the age of 101, sculptor/potter Beatrice Wood is full of ideas for new and different kinds of pots and producing what one critic calls "strong, beautiful works that are probably the best of her career." Known for her lustreware-pottery with a glass-like glazed surface that shifts colors when viewed from different angles-and her "Naughty Figures" (Example: "Marriage"—two primitive faces, a man and a woman, side by side, radiating unhappiness), Wood has shocked and delighted the art world for over 60 years.

Recently, on a misty fall afternoon, she relaxed in her home/studio overlooking Southern California's gold-green Ojai Valley. Wrapped in a pink and turquoise sari accented by heavy silver bracelets and glitsy rings and earrings, Wood glows with an inner light as clear as her famous lustre glazes. Perhaps her good friend Anais Nin summed up Wood's magic when she once remarked: "Water poured from one of her jars will taste like wine."

JNB: Is it true that you became a potter because you couldn't find a teapot to match some plates you'd bought?

BW: Yes. I'd bought some lustre plates in Holland. And I told an actor friend of mine, "I can't find a teapot to match my set." And he said, "There's a class at Hollywood High School. Go there and make one." So the next day I went, intending to make a teapot over the weekend. It's incomprehensible to me today that I was so stupid!

JNB: What happened when you tried to fashion the teapot?

BW: Well, of course I couldn't. I couldn't do anything with the clay-it was such a strange medium! So instead of the teapot, I made a little clay figure-and somebody bought it for $2.50. So I made another figure and somebody else bought that one. So I thought, "Maybe I'll go back to that class and make little figures. Maybe I can make ten dollars a month." It was the height of the depression and I was living on sixty-three dollars a month, so ten dollars was a beautiful amount!

JNB: Did you feel clumsy when you first began working with clay?

BW: I didn't feel related to it. I studied with Glen Lukens, who had a craft school, and I was the worst student in the class. It wasn't natural for me to work with clay. That's why I say that I'm an artist in clay, rather than a craftsman.

JNB: What felt unnatural about it?

BW: Look, take cooking. Take two women: One will make delicious things and another will make dull things from the same recipe. I'm not naturally a craftsman.

JNB: Did you study with anyone else besides Lukens?

BW: When I read that Otto and Gertrude Natzler had arrived in Los Angeles from Germany, I wrote them and asked if they wanted a student. They approached [making pots] from a standpoint of beauty-not just making masses of clay. They took me [as a student] and then, somehow, an agent got a hold of me. And before I knew it, I was a potter.

JNB: Did you ever go to art school?

BW: Just for three months in Paris, when I was 15 years old.

JNB: Who would you say influenced you the most?

BW: In clay, Glen Lukens and the Natzlers, and I took a few lessons from Viveka and Otto Heino. And then there's this wonderful potter from Hawaii, Toshiko Takaezu, who makes beautiful pots. One day she sat down at the wheel and showed me a new way of centering the clay, because I was having trouble.

JNB: Did you study other people's work?

BW: Yes. I exposed myself to all the pottery I could see—all the museums, all the magazines, all the pictures. Because everything we see has impact on us. When I was a child, my parents took me to Europe and dragged me and my governess through museums. The lustreware I saw there made an unconscious impact on me. When I became a potter, those images came back, and that was what I wanted to do.

JNB: You're known for your unique glazes. How do you create them?

BW: I'm not a chemist but I do use a formula. Either a colleague has given me one, or I take one published in a magazine and I do things to it. For example: As a young bride, I want to make a sauce for vegetables-a little bit of butter, cheese, salt. All right. But maybe I'll add some mustard and double the cheese-and before I know it, I've taken the basic formula and transformed it. And that's what I do with my glazes. . I don't understand it.

You can achieve beautiful lustres through what is called 'reduction firing.' That's when you smoke your kiln and the smoke moving around touches the glazes and transforms them. That's the way I work.

Let's say you put some toast in [the toaster] for a few minutes and it comes out nice. But what if you put that toast in [a kiln] and you smoke your kiln so that you overfire it? The toast will come out transformed-it'll be burnt and dark. Smoking the kiln causes changes, at the right temperature, but it's very tricky because you can't control how the smoke is going to move. It changes every time—but that's what makes it interesting.

JNB: You've said that every time you open the kiln it's a surprise.

BW: And many times I have nothing but disasters! The last kiln I had, not one piece came out to please me.

JNB: When you complete a piece, are you often not happy with it?

BW: I'm rarely happy with it! It rarely comes out as I visualized it.

JNB: Are you hard on yourself?

BW: I hope so! That'll keep me improving. I'm not too happy with what I do·when it's done. My joy is in doing it. Yesterday I walked into a friend's house and saw a little bowl I'd given him for his birthday and I said, "My God, that's good! I wish I hadn't given it to you."

JNB: Why do you think you appreciate your work more when some time has elapsed?

BW: Because I look at it free of what I imagined. I've forgotten what I visualized, so I see it without hope, without judgment.

JNB: You were active in the avant-garde movement after World War I. And yet you once said that the first time you saw modern art it looked like "scrawls." What made you change your view?

BW: One night I went to the home of the Arensbergs, who were very famous collectors in the painting world. The door opened, these two nice people met me and behind them were these terrible wild paintings. And I said to myself, "If I'm going to keep up a friendship with these people, I'll have to understand what all this is about."

So one evening I sat and looked at a Matisse, a very famous painter. He had this figure with these lines around it. And I looked and looked and looked…And suddenly it became beautiful. And that was the opening to me of what modern art is all about.

JNB: Would you say you're still judgmental at times?

BW: I'm a snob about art because as a child my eyes were attuned to great paintings. Forty-eight years ago, I was asked to be a judge at the Ventura County (CA) fair. And there were eight little figures from the same mold—one red, one blue, one green. And I said, "I can't judge things from the same mold." And a woman took me aside and said, "That's not the way to look at it. This is the first gesture towards aesthetics by the rancher's wife. So judge it from that standpoint."

Then three months ago, I said to a colleague, "It's a waste of time to teach high school children pottery for an hour-and-a-half, twice a week. You can't make anything good in that time." And she said, "That's not the purpose. It awakens them to aesthetics." And that is so important.

JNB: Isn't that exactly what happened to you when you discovered pottery through that class at Hollywood High School?

BW: Yes. It awakened me to beauty, to the creative opportunities in clay.

JNB: What does it feel like to be 100 years old?

BW: I'm asked that continually. A little boy of 10 asked me and I said, "What does it feel like to be 10?" That's the answer. I'm totally unconscious of being 100. I don't think about it at all. I say to people, "All right, I'm 100 to you, but to me I'm 32." I never think, "I'm 100—I shouldn't throw at the wheel." When I was in my workroom this morning, it never occurred to me that I'm a 100-year-old bag and I should go more slowly. No. I just thought, "Oh, I must get this clay started."

JNB: Have you noticed any change in your sense of time?

BW: I have a bookkeeper who comes once a week, and it seems to me that it's only two days that he's away. Before I know it, he's back and the week is gone. It's very strange.

JNB: Some people feel that time is speeding up. . .

BW: Particularly when you're busy!

JNB: Have you had any health difficulties that have restricted your work?

BW: I have an old woman's back-I'm willing, out of courtesy, to say that to you. But to me, it's a bad back. That's different.

JNB: What's an 'old woman'?

BW: A woman who loses her interest in young men! In a way, the back problem has been a blessing because it's forced me to focus. [Without it] I'd be much more active. I have such an interest in the world and what's going on that I'd be here and there. But it's been very hard.

JNB: What causes your back pain?

BW: When I was younger, I had very difficult times: I married the wrong type of man and I was without money. So I'd go around with my neck and shoulders tightened and my neck vertebrae kind of grew together. And for years there has been this exhaustion from the pressure. I'm still not free of it. But I have acupuncture treatments and I'm much better today than I was two years ago.

JNB: Speaking of men, you've said that you "never loved the jerks you married and never married the men you loved." Why was that?

BW: I've bad luck with men because I'm a monogamous woman in a polygamous world. I was brought up that way, you see. When I was a little girl, I had this dream that a marvelous knight on a white horse would grab me and we'd live happily together forever after. I still think it's a wonderful dream, but reality's not like that. So I make pottery.

JNB: Do you think it's necessary to be unhappy or dissatisfied to create good art?

BW: If you've been a happy person all your life, I don't think there's this push to be an artist. Art is kind of a neurotic activity. It's all consuming. And we artists are self-interested. If you're a great artist, all you think about is "my art." I have to watch myself because I could just forget all about people, all about the world. But that's not the way to live. Art comes from blockages. You put your blockage into the song of art.

JNB: Did you ever feel severely blocked—as if you couldn't create?

BW: No, never. I never thought in those ways.

JNB: What advice would you offer artists and potters?

BW: I can only say "Work." Nothing has ever been achieved without hard work. Whatever success I've had has all been from self-discipline. I work whether or not I'm tired. When I have a commitment, I keep it. I don't go away for the weekend with a young or an old man. And my work is ready when I say I will deliver.

And pay attention to your invoices. I once delivered pottery to a large department store and the manager said, "Where's your invoice?" I said, "What's an invoice?" And she said, "It's a list." So I said, "Madam, I am an <u>artist</u>; I don't make lists!" And she said, "Then how do you expect to get paid?"

That was a revolution in my life. Since then my invoices have been perfect. Three museums have said they're the best they've ever had. So I say: Be professional. Have your invoices in order because it's part of the business side.

JNB: What would you say to those who are struggling to make a living through their art?

BW: If you're a true artist, you will keep on, but don't do it to make money. Many people go into crafts to have exhibitions or to make money. It's not from the heart, so there's a lot of stuff made that's not interesting at all.

JNB: Your career has spanned over 60 years. Why do you think you've been so successful?

BW: I'm curious. Curiosity is vital. And that's why I keep working with lustres, because I never know how the kiln is going to turn out.

JNB: Do you still experiment?

BW: Continually. I'm working now on a large decorative soup tureen. I'm not sure how I'm going to glaze it, but I keep thinking that I could ruin it with the wrong glaze.

JNB: Would you take that risk?

BW: Oh, yes! I could use a certain glaze that I'm sure of and it would come out, certainly. But what I see in my imagination—if I can attain it—the tureen will be really beautiful and interesting. And I'm going to take that chance.

The Gathering of the Grandmothers

The purpose of our coming together as a collective consciousness is to teach, empower and support women in the process of aging. In many societies, elders are viewed as the wise women of the community. They are revered, respected and sought after for their counsel, advice and teaching. Their view of the past and wisdom gained in years lived on earth earns them their place as an elder. By acknowledging and integrating the eldering process in our consciousness, the value of life for all generations becomes enriched and promotes necessary multigenerational communication.

With others of similar interests, we Grandmothers are consciously celebrating our coming of age. We learn to grow old creatively with joyous anticipation, positive understanding and newfound honor and respect for our role in society.

The Grandmothers Group weaves women's history, heritage, spirituality and culture in new ways. We recognize and celebrate women's vast and integral contributions to family, community, society and our own aging process.

The Hopi Prophecy states, "When the Grandmothers speak, the Earth will heal."

We are taking the responsibility to be that voice!

Malka Golden-Wolfe

WHEN THE GRANDMOTHERS SPEAK

Lynne Namka (author credit)

Never doubt that a group of thoughtful committed citizens can change the world.

Margaret Mead

Older women are the Weaver Women, who live long enough to plan out the warp and woof of the fabric of their lives. One by one, each one of us in turn weaves out the stories of our life as our truth bids us do. We help keep Universal Truth alive by passing on the mysteries of being a woman. We are the Bridge Builders reaching out and showing men new and different ways to live. Our bridge crosses gender duality, hopefully so that the future generations of men and women can live without separatism. We women can share compassion with what Robert Bly calls "that great hairy, musty tribe."

All women's stories are interconnected, just as our lives are interconnected. In telling our stories, we become strong. And thus we become authentic. And in doing so, we strengthen others. In playing out the ancient stories, we come home. And encourage others to seek their own unique journey home. Toni Packward said it well: "You are the book. The most important book to read is yourself. If you read that book, you will have read all others." If we are discerning, diligent and perhaps very lucky, we learn to trust the process of whatever is presented to us.

Those lively story spirits are with us tonight as the fire burns, flares, snorts, and hisses. The story spirits of fire have their own stories to tell. They call out to you. Can you hear the ancient spirits as they beckon you to come forward? Since ancient times women have come together to share their stories of wisdom, aging and healing. Now it is your turn. Now it is time for you to add your own story to those of time immemorial. Elder women coming together to aid in the healing of the world? Ahhh, listen well...

GRANDMOTHER CRONES OFFER SOLUTIONS AND HOPE

"If we listen with our hearts we can hear."

Jan Gregg

The images we watch every night on the news leave us overwhelmed in despair—faces etched with pain and desperation in Bosnia, enormous eyes of starving children in northern Africa, hands flung to the air by grieving mothers and widows of the Middle East. The injustices and violence of our own country leave us at a loss as well—how can such unmitigated evil be fought by those of us just struggling to get by and raise our families'? Kindness and gentleness are usually met with hostility and anger. Helplessness in the face of the maelstrom of despair of our era seems to be the only sensible or meaningful response.

There was a woman who lived on a small ranch in southern Arizona who said that the world did not have to be that way, and that a life lived well by any mindful individual has the power to change others. Her name was Mary Diamond, and she proved it by using her retirement years to offer peace and hope through the power of individuals coming together to bring solutions to the world's problems. Diamond was the founder of the Grandmother movement.

Diamond has spent the five years building Cielo en Tierra, a small ranch outside Huachuca City, Ariz. This ranch, utilizing nontraditional building techniques and experimental approaches to living off the land, was the result of a vision Diamond had in her middle 60's. In 1993, Mary had another vision in which she was told—"I don't know how, I was just told"—that she should call together women of her own age to meet and share their distress and perhaps find answers to the dilemmas of the era. Having worked for many years with Native Americans, Diamond knew such messages were to be taken seriously, and she planned such a conference. The first Grandmothers Gathering was held at Cielo en Tierra in 1994, during the full moon of October. "My vision was very clear; the gatherings should always be held at that time," Diamond said. The sixteen women who attended shared their pain as well as possibilities for change in the world.

Beautiful words from the Creator
When he created us—each one he created.
He gave us a spirit, connected to us.
To talk to us, guide us.
The beautiful words we don't hear with our ears.
If we listen with our hearts we can hear.
We can be guided by Him

If we listen.
The world would be a better place
If we all listen to Him.
His words are so beautiful;
His words are more precious than silver or gold.
It's free!

It was with this prayer in her own language sung by Sylvia Wallulatum, a Native American elder from the Pacific Northwest, that the Grandmothers Gathering opened on October 6, 1995 at the Biosphere near Tucson, Ariz. When she concluded her prayer song, Wallulatum shared the grief she felt in dealing with the Native American young people who had lost their way in a complicated world. She said she believed that leaving the old ways—the foods and customs of the old times, the understanding of the rhythms of nature—was depleting the young people's ability to develop satisfying lives. "We elders have talked many times about what we can do for our young people—it's very discouraging, especially now that the area tribes have decided to build a casino. The elders were against it, and we are looking for ways to try to explain to the young people saying that there were other ways." Then this fragile, beautiful woman in her eighties, and in a wheelchair, transcended age and culture with her solution: "I was looking for a grant," she said, "That will provide a way for us to make videos of prisoners with long-term convictions, telling the children that their way was the wrong way. The prisoners have already agreed to it—they believe it is something positive they can do."

The Grandmothers meeting attracted over sixty-five women from all over the world, from a myriad of lifestyles and an array of professions. There were 60's hippies, well-dressed professional women, and down-to-earth Mom types. The differences faded away as the meetings progressed and friendships were formed. All shared the conviction that, like Sylvia Wallulatum, they have the power to change the world.

These energetic and happy women bore no resemblance to the pathetic and self-absorbed oldsters we've come to expect from TV and movies—there was not a mention of aches and pains, facelifts or disappointing men. These women spoke of their latest projects, the trip being planned, the next book to be written.

When turning to the reason for the gathering, the conversation became discouraged, but stayed optimistic. There was great sadness in discussion of the turmoil and pain young people are suffering everywhere. There was alarm in hearing of the women's conference in China—a participant described the pervasive coal dust that covered the landscape and, with the one-child policy, that there were fewer baby girls was evident.

There was also hope at the Grandmothers Gathering. The women who felt themselves called to this meeting responded to something much greater than could be explained verbally. These women—far past childbearing, past earning a living, past the compulsive need to couple—had great gifts to share. Some described their work with inner city children. One described her retirement at fifty—living in a tent, without car or possessions, and traveling across North and South America to assist in building construction and program development for the disadvantaged. Two women well into their eighties described their dance performances. A "young" woman of fifty-two talked about her publication called *The Crone Chronicles.* These women had lived through it all, and had arrived on the other side strong, powerful, and aware of their gifts.

Of the gathering, Diamond said, "Our goal was to double the participation of the first year—we had sixteen attend. That we had sixty-five participants this year is beyond my wildest imagination! It means, of course, that the gathering is meeting a strong need that older women are feeling. It's a hunger to come together and share our concerns and possibly solutions. Every woman who has come here has been called. We're here to do something important—as yet we just don't know what that is." When asked about the plans for the 1996 Grandmother's Gathering, Diamond said, "We've only had a rough agenda of what we were going to do this year, but there's been a purpose here, an unfolding. There have been so many diverse talents here; things have really begun to happen. I see each year as totally different. I see it as becoming more global, as it was originally intended to be in my vision. We've been invited to have the gathering in England next year, and again, we expect it to double in size.

"I would like to see us get more specific in ways we can help children. I would like to see a group of young women and girls attend as representatives of The Maiden, giving them a chance to see The Crone talk about how wonderful life can be in this stage. I would like to see representatives from all groups—the Maiden, the Mother, as well as the Crone—come together to learn and share their ideas to improve things. There is real depth of caring in the women who are participating and we need to respond to that."

An Anthem to Our Global Family

The Grandmothers at Cielo en Tierra

Yes, life!
What color are your tears?
Please come to the peaceful circle
to listen to the Grandmothers
for it is time, it is time.
In Light and Trust, take our hand, United
Just listen, listen, listen.
Stay conscious and keep the magic, wonder, mystery
We will not be put on a shelf.
The Grandmothers hold the essential.
Walk in beauty, wise women
Dance and sing and make life poem
together, together!
All Grandmothers awaken to oneness
Straighten this crooked house
Catch the things that are falling
All is divine. All is One
Come as a child,
Come as a third son
Come as the third daughter,
Come in all things to rejoin.
We come in as Maidens, Mothers and Crones
We complete the cycle
All, respect us,

We give birth to the next cycle
Don't be afraid of silence, of death
The Grandmothers stand at the doorway to death and rebirth
Watch us,
Witches who hold each other together with out feet
A firm foundation between heaven and earth!
We are setting our feet to the task
Read through your feet as they touch our mother sky!

COUNCIL OF GRANDMOTHERS

Gaia Reblitz

"Do you know a Grandmother who has lived her life in tradition, light, joy, spirituality and wisdom? It is time again for a gathering of such women!" So began Mary Diamond's letter of invitation to the second Council of Grandmothers. The meeting took place at the Biosphere near Tucson in Arizona, at the full moon of October.

The year before, sixteen Grandmothers had gathered at Mary's retreat "Cielo en Tierra" (Heaven on Earth), to lay the foundation and light the flame for such a Council, inspired by the Native American prophecy: "When the Grandmothers speak, the Earth will heal.' Grave concern about our children and our planet, about the disregard for Feminine wisdom in the world and the silencing of age found voice in a proclamation to the public and President Clinton. With it the request was made that 1995 be declared the "Year of the Grandmother." White House and Congress responded promptly, but with a typical amendment: 1995 became the official *"Year of the Grandparent."* More than sixty Grandmothers met at this year's Council, ranging in age from barely 50 to almost 100. Some represented Native American tribes; one came from Germany and one from the Celtic tradition in England.

Not all of us have grandchildren of our own. But we all had entered the gate of menopause and been initiated into wise womanhood. That meant, we are finally growing into our true selves and reaching out into the world with love, compassion, courage and freedom of spirit. Each of us is still active in our community-as spiritual leader, healer, teacher, counselor, dancer, artist or organizer. Proud to be crones, to be conscious elders, we are breaking the stereotype about "the old woman" so that the world will honor and receive again the blessings of Grandmother wisdom.

In all traditions, which we represented at the council, wise elder women had stood at the center of a community, keepers of their people's vision and heritage, gentle teachers and loving guides, peacemakers and counselors. They had watched out for the children, for younger women and for our Earth Mother. Aware of the power of circles and cycles, they had nurtured ceremonies and rituals, initiations and celebrations, so that the sacredness and joy of everyday life would be affirmed. Through these wise Grandmothers spoke the mature voice of the heart. When that voice becomes silent or is discounted, a society sickens and dies.

The Council of Grandmothers, marked by great love and respect for each other and a warm, embracing intelligence, turned into a four-day ceremony and celebration. The program started as a bare outline, so that the vast talents of the group could fill it. We began our mornings with meditation and a dance to the four directions. Before each meal, we held hands in a great circle to give thanks to life and to strengthen our bond with each other. Workshops centered on healing ways and realignment with nature's cycles, on activism and community work, on our long line of feminine tradition, on ways to create sacred space.

Ceremonies bound us together as one, with song and dance and prayer, with Shamanic journeying and Full Moon ritual. One special afternoon, the younger ones sat, in a circle around our true Elders to listen to their stories and counsel. Silently surrounding them with our love and respect, we remembered how good it feels to honor again the wisdom of the Old ones.

Our small delegation from Oregon had the privilege to bring Grandmother Sylvia Wallulatum from the Warm Springs tribe down to Arizona. Her gentle and powerful presence touched everyone in the Council. Sitting in a wheelchair in ceremonial dress, she listened and shared with great kindness and dignity, humor and humility. As the daughter of a chief, before the U.S. government imposed modern tribal councils, she had been raised traditionally and in service to her people. To this day she works very hard to keep the sacred ways of her tribe alive. She shared a special gift, a ceremonial laughing song and dance. While it was lots of fun, it cleansed and healed us and reminded us that everything we do can be a ceremony and a prayer.

The gathering ended with the establishment of a traveling council of thirteen grandmothers (one for each moon of the year). As a group or individually, they will visit different states to spread the message, to meet with Elders and organizations, to create a network of communication and action.

As more than 40 million women in the U.S. stand at the threshold of menopause, daughters of the postwar baby boom, there is a new awareness rising about aging, about the way of the Feminine and the power of sisterhood. Women of all ages are redefining who they are. May they bring back to the world their holy gifts as maiden, mother and crone.

WISE WOMEN ON SPIRITUALITY

Women need to know their sacredness. We are the bowl of the pipe. We are the carriers of the fire that sends the messages. We cannot be complete without the stem of the pipe. We are earth and stone together. The bowl of the pipe is made from stone. The herbs of the earth are smoked within. Women need to use the medicine of laughter in all they do. Women need to honor themselves and become aware of their sacredness.

Donna Buseman

"To the possession of thyself the way is inward," says Plotinus. "The cell of self-knowledge is the stall in which the pilgrim must be reborn," says St. Catherine of Siena.... Woman must be the pioneer in this turning inward for strength. In a sense, she has always been the pioneer.

Anne Morrow Lindbergh

A woman invents her life around a man because it is expected and because it also suits her, only to discover that "insufficiency of spirit." We learn that we must become more than we've been, not because it is The Answer, or Nirvana, but because we really have no choice. There is no Happily Ever After. We grow, before and after, in paradox and in contradiction. But as we grow—if nothing else—whatever we may lose, we gain ourselves: a marvelous hedge against living alone.

Iris Sangiuliano

We do die a little with each ruptured innocence. We do pay the price for that irresistible desire to know ourselves, and subsequently the other, more intimately. We take that sometimes-painful passage from dependency to responsibility from innocence to knowledge and phoenix—like, we rise again from the ashes.

Iris Sangiuliano

The true self-sacrifice is the one that sacrifices the hidden thing in the self, which would work harm to ourselves and to others. It is an effort to become more and more conscious of all the forces in the unconscious, of the unworthy personal motives that work underground, as well as the inherited forces, so that our lives shall become more and more full of understanding and of really conscious choice. In this way we do "descend into hell," the depth of the unconscious where lies all those things that would destroy our conscious attitude and which we most fear to face and acknowledge.

Learn to get in touch with the silence within yourself and know that everything in this life has a purpose... There is no need to go to India or anywhere else to find peace. You will find that deep place of silence right in your room, your garden, or even your bathtub.

Elisabeth Kubler-Ross

One must be able to strip oneself of all self-deception, to see oneself naked to one's own eyes before one can come to terms with the elements of oneself and know who one really is.

Frances G. Wickes

CLAN MOTHER

Gaia Reblitz

A life consciously lived
in tradition and service,
in great humility
and full responsibility.
Her arms around her people
she accepts everyone
into her heart
and her prayer's protection.
She knows each one
· as a part of the circle,
weaving family
out of fraying strands.
Each new generation
she welcomes to life
and for those passing over
she opens the stargate.
Girls learn from her
to be fully woman,
To know mystery and magic,
to live sacred and whole.
And boys she teaches
in games and through stories
how to protect and respect
themselves and all others.

She is a keeper of spirit,
a voice for love and peace,
a woman of vision,
a tool for universal laws.
She knows many worlds,
looks behind the veils,
keeps Earth and Sky aligned
and prays for all she sees.
A center of quiet,
joining laughter and tears,
she walks ever so lightly
on her beloved earth.
In council meet with her,
Hear her voice in yourself,
honor and love her,
and blessed be your world.

OATH OF THE CLAN MOTHERS

Joyce Kovelman

As I embrace and enfold the
Sacredness of Clan Motherhood
I join with my Sisters and Grandmothers
in declaration.
We say Yes to Joy
We say Yes to Love
We say Yes to Peace
 And we serve as Midwives
 To the healing of Mother Earth
 and Father Sky.

THE GRANDMOTHERS SPEAK

For the first time in history, enormous numbers of women are traveling through the gate of menopause and looking forward to a life span of some 30 more years. And we women have a certain hard-won wisdom, gleaned through consciously processing the experiences of our long and fruitful lives. What are we going to do with this wisdom? Play golf? Get our hair done? We begin to glimpse the opportunity, and the responsibility.

Ann Kreilkamp

Grandmothers are very important. Grandmothers are the hub of the sacred hoop. They are beacons of light saying, "This is where you are going."

Mahisha

An evolution in consciousness has begun, carrying with it the seeds of new personhood. A new Self strives to grow outwardly into space and time. In the deeper recesses of consciousness, there are not better or worse parts of the Self; all are expressions of the Whole. The seed and the tree are understood as one and the same, both being aspects of an event occurring over space and time.

Joyce Kovelman

We are coming into a time of the woman again. We are entering this time of change. My reason for being in the world is to become the best

192 • A Gathering of Grandmothers

woman I can possibly become. What I do inside sets the stage for outward change in the world. I start in my inner room and go outward—to my house, to my garden, to my community and to the world.

Vivien Mayer

As Grandmothers, we know that Aging is a process of Transcendence and of releasing the physical and material. Through this process of releasing, a space of emptiness opens, allowing Universe to fill us with joy, serenity and peace. We Grandmothers are the heralds of a new spirituality upon Earth. We urge all of humankind to support our growth and inner awakening, and to help us usher in an era of Peace on Earth and Peace with Earth.

Joyce Kovelman

Being an older woman means that I live my life as an example. Now I don't have so much responsibility to my children and grandchildren. I am a contributor to myself, and I take care of myself. I have things to give back, as I've been given so much. It's time for me to give back, and Hospice is my way of giving back. I like my life. I like this age. I'm no longer in the age of acquisition. I have all I need. I'm carefree. I'm unencumbered.

Phyllis Fredona

As the momentum of global change intensifies, we are each challenged to live from the depths of our soul and offer our utmost to each other and to the well being of this planet.

Gay Luce

THE ART OF LIFE

Joanna Miller

I don't know what the grief is, but I do know it is grief. To cry—to let it be—is all I can do. I just come into the pain and look at it softly and gently and weep when ready with tears. I release the flow of sadness in a loving way to soften the hard edges of loss and terror. And in the process, I know a transformation occurs and the mystery of rebirth manifests itself in most profound and unexpected ways.

Life is on all levels: birthing, living and dying. Everything is as transitional as the shedding of the serpent's skin. Life without its cycles does not exist. The art of life is to know that death truly makes birth possible and to yield to that continuous process.

Like all art, life calls forth intuitive knowing and trust that this is what is holy. One lives in the quest and the uncertainty of the process as it is given to us from within. One lives with the unwillingness to be in the unknown and uncomfortable space. And so one opens to the gift of the mystery tremendous.

WISDOM WITHIN

Mary Ann McClellan

Unfolding our total spiritual potential is the only realistic solution remaining for the personal and global problems facing us. In providing teachings that open the doorway to our true selves, we will provide a connection to our true identity. I believe that the feminine nature is wisdom itself—the most direct path to realization—the tool to Enlightenment. Our feminine nature gives birth or creates our own reality—we are all mothers of reality. The feminine nature never lies dormant; it is always birthing. Woman's nature, no matter what her age, is the fertile ground that is always producing.

By learning about the "Moon Time" ways of old, women begin to realize the awesome respect they must have for their bodies. In doing so, women will begin to realize the power that they carry within and the responsibility toward themselves that this represents. We have all the answers we seek within us. The Universe and Creation reflect perfection to us. When we look to Nature, we find a perfect reflection of all that is. Our bodies, being part of Nature, afford us with the teachings.

It is only in coming together, in collective consciousness, that our responsibility in this life will be fulfilled. We chose to come in female bodies to do the work of this era. We wise women have passed through the flowering stage, into full bloom, and are now ready to pass on the seeds for a future of peace, love and harmony. May our hearts be truly open now!

GRANDMOTHER'S WAY

In honor of the Dineh/Navajo Way of Life

Gaia Reblitz

She brings down the Sky
to her sacred Earth
with blessings
from Rainbow Woman.
Lightning is the sacred fire,
thunder the Spirit's voice,
moon her never forgotten sister,
star a timeless relative.
Grandmother's heart
holds the whole
of the universe.
Her people still sing
the songs of creation.
Caretakers they are
of Earth Mother's beauty,
weaving the rhythms of ceremonies
into a pattern of healing
and survival.
Grandmother knows.
As the corn pollen
falls from her hands,

an offering,
a prayer.
a blessing,
the balance of life continues.

ANCIENT PROPHECY

Lynne Namka

"When the Grandmothers speak, the Earth will heal."

You are a woman of wisdom.
You have become so by the living of your story,
the experiencing of your losses,
the knowing of your deepest feelings.
Your wisdom has come from going deep within
to find your true being.
You walk a sacred path while here on this earth.
You hold a sacred responsibility
to those caught in disharmony,
to the children
to yourself.
To all.
Wise woman, speak out with compassion.
Speak out wise woman.
Take your voice and speak out.
Speak out about truth that is pure.
Speak out about loving those who do not know love.
Speak out about giving to those in need.
About treating all in this great green earth with respect.
Speak out about the horrors of war and the joys of peace.
Take your wise knowing voice.
Send it throughout our land.

Say what needs to be said.
Say what needs to be heard.
Women all, speaking out in a collective voice.
The power of one magnified by the power of many.
Women coming together in wisdom and power.
Women, beautiful women, all ages, colors, shapes, sizes
Speaking out to change our world.

So Sisters dear, come closer, closer while the story spirits begin their tales of what did happen to our planet when the Grandmothers spoke their wisdom.

Ahhh, but that is another story...

0-595-23990-0

Printed in the United Kingdom
by Lightning Source UK Ltd.
98682UKS00001B/47